THE
PERSON AND MINISTRY

OF THE

HOLY SPIRIT.

EDITED BY

A. C. DIXON,

PASTOR OF THE IMMANUEL BAPTIST CHURCH
BALTIMORE, MD.

———

WIPF & STOCK · Eugene, Oregon

Wipf and Stock Publishers
199 W 8th Ave, Suite 3
Eugene, OR 97401

The Person and Ministry of the Holy Spirit
By Dixon, A. C.
ISBN 13: 978-1-5326-4630-0
Publication date 12/28/2017
Previously published by Wharton, Barron & Co., 1890

EXPLANATORY.

WHILE the writer was evangelizing in Europe, he received a letter from his friend, A. C. Dixon, of Baltimore, requesting his help in organizing and supervising a Conference in that city. On my return home Mr. Dixon visited me, and together we sketched the programme of the subjects, nominated speakers, and arranged concerning dates and details. On Mr. Dixon's return to Baltimore he consulted with the pastors, who, with him, formed a committee to prosecute the work in the city. To this earnest committee is due, under God, the great success which crowned the Convention.

The pleasant task of correspondence with speakers and adjustment of subjects fell to my lot, as on other similar occasions. Many brethren, originally appointed to present the subjects, were detained in various ways, but others cheerfully undertook the office of teacher. The promise, "Them that honour Me I will honour," sustained our faith, and God permitted our ears to hear marvelous things throughout this four days' meeting.

The following is the text of the circular letter, which explains itself:

Bible Schools, Christian Conventions, and Theological Conferences have been multiplying themselves, of late years, throughout this and other lands. The result has been a revived interest in Bible Study, and a more Scriptural method of preaching and teaching the Divine Word on the part of pastors, evangelists, and other fellow-laborers.

Many of these Conferences and Conventions have been of a special character, notably those held in New York and Chicago for the consideration of Prophetic Themes, and that held in Philadelphia for the vindication of Bible Inspiration.

It is now thought best to hold a Four Days' Meeting in the City of Baltimore, where THE GLORIOUS PERSON AND MANIFOLD MINISTRY OF THE HOLY SPIRIT shall form the subject of teaching. The invitation comes from a number of Pastors who cordially invite their fellow-Christians of every name to assemble with them during the four days commencing with Tuesday, October 29th. Many of the speakers who took part in previous Conferences, in addition to well-known Pastors and

EXPLANATORY.

Seminary Professors, will present carefully prepared addresses on this vital theme.

That there is a tendency to practically ignore the Presence and Ministry of the Spirit in the professing church is painfully noticeable. To warn against this declension and to recall believers to a more practical recognition of His presence and relations to the church, and the world, is the object aimed at in thus calling together the disciples of our Lord. Carnality in the church or in the individual can only be met and overcome by an increase of, and an intensity of the Holy Spirit's Ministry in our midst.

The Conference will be inter-denominational, and an expression of the vital union of believers with one another in Jesus Christ.

Names of speakers, hours of sessions, and place of meeting will be duly announced.

GEO. C. NEEDHAM,
A. C. DIXON,
On behalf of Committee.

JOHN F. PULLEN, Treasurer,
    12 East Fayette Street.

The Convention was held in the Mt. Vernon Place M. E. Church, Baltimore, and the attendance upon all the sessions was very large. Its four days were days of heaven upon earth.

At one time no less than one hundred ministers requested prayer for the fullness of the Holy Ghost. Appeals have come from other cities for like Conferences, but as yet we have been too much occupied with evangelistic labors to comply with the request. We purpose, D. V., when opportunity offers, to multiply such meetings for the consideration and elucidation of this great theme—The Person and Work of the Holy Spirit.

Mr. Dixon, in editing the book, has thought it best to publish the addresses just as they were furnished by the speakers. Such repetitions as have occurred are necessary to a full understanding of the subject in hand. They are now sent forth in the present form with much prayer that the gift of power through the indwelling of the Spirit may rest upon every reader.

Geo. C. Needham.

Elim Cottage,
Manchester-by-the-Sea, Mass.

CONTENTS.

		PAGE
I.	INTRODUCTION	1
	By A. C. Dixon.	
II.	ADDRESS OF WELCOME	9
	By Bishop A. W. Wilson.	
III.	THE HOLY SPIRIT THE REVEALER OF CHRIST .	12
	By Rev. George S. Bishop, D.D.	
IV.	THE ENDUEMENT OF THE SPIRIT	37
	By Rev. Julius E. Grammar, D D.	
V.	THE SPIRIT'S THREEFOLD CONVICTION	48
	By Rev. George Dana Boardman, D D., LL.D.	
VI.	ADDRESS BY REV. M. D. BABCOCK	66
VII.	THE SPIRIT OF SONSHIP	70
	By Rev. W. J. Erdman.	
VIII.	THE HEAVENLY UNCTION	77
	By Rev. L. W. Munhall, D.D.	
IX.	GRIEVING, TEMPTING, RESISTING THE SPIRIT .	86
	By Rev. James Morrow, D.D.	
X.	THE SPIRIT FOR WORSHIP AND WITNESSING ..	102
	By Rev. D M. Stearns	
XI.	THE SPIRIT IN AGREEMENT WITH THE WORD .	117
	By Rev W. J. Erdman	
XII.	THE HOLY SPIRIT AND THE CHRISTIAN	124
	By Rev. F. M. Ellis, D.D.	
XIII.	THE SPIRIT OF PROPHECY	150
	By Bishop W. R. Nicholson, D.D.	

THE PERSON AND MINISTRY

OF THE

HOLY SPIRIT.

I.

INTRODUCTION.

BY A. C. DIXON.

THE Spirit of God came on the day of Pentecost, as the rushing mighty wind and the tongues of flame; and from that day to this he has been with his people. We sometimes pray that he may be poured out upon us; let us rather strive to realize that he is already with us, and what we need is to appropriate this ever present power. He is not weaker to-day, and stronger to-morrow, but "the same yesterday, to-day and forever." Omnipotence dwelling with his people, ready to work through them. The practical question, then, is, How can this ever present personal power be appropriated? Through a threefold channel.

INTRODUCTION.

1. We read in Hebrews 11, the muster-roll of God's mighty ones. The secret of their power was FAITH. "According to your faith be it unto you," is a law never to be changed. Faith is the connecting wire between the battery of God's power and the hearts of men. We look at the swift current of Niagara Falls and strive to imagine what a force it would be, if utilized in manufacture or in generating electricity. God's power is like the Niagara current, always the same, to be turned for the accomplishment of his purpose by the channels of Christian faith. When New York harbor was to be deepened, a mine of dynamite was placed beneath it; the engineer took his little daughter, and told her to place her finger upon the knob, and by the weight of her hand the electric current was made to flash under the channel and shake all New York by the explosion. The engineer might have touched that knob himself; but it was his wish that his child should do it. God could do without our help, but it is his desire and plan that his people by the touch of faith should let loose his omnipotence.

2. But hand in hand with faith must go the WORD. The Spirit uses his own sword, the "Word of God;" and when we substitute our words for his, we substitute weakness for strength. "Where the word of a king is, there is power." Eccl. 8 : 4. "The voice of the Lord is powerful." Ps. 29 : 4. We are as Aaron, taking the words of God and delivering them to the people. Our words may be like the sheet lightning, beautiful

and grand, but sheet lightning never strikes anything. God's Word is the forked flash that strikes down the towers of sin. Our words are, at the best, only unconfined steam, making fog and confusion; God's Word is the steam within the cylinder that drives the piston and carries forward his work.

"A brilliant operation that is," said a French physician; "I have performed it many a time." "How many patients lived?" asked an inquirer. "Oh, they all died," replied the boastful physician; "but the operation was very brilliant." We perform brilliant oratorical operations, giving our words which kill to the people, when we ought to be giving God's Word, which imparts life. "Get thee unto the house of Israel," said the Lord to Ezekiel, "and speak ye my words unto them." He obeyed, and Israel trembled. Let us heed the same command, and the people will be moved.

3. There must also be character. "The eyes of the Lord run to and fro throughout the whole earth, to show himself strong in the behalf of them whose heart is perfect toward him." 2 Chron. 16 : 9. Care little for reputation, what men may think of us; care everything for character, what God thinks of us. He is looking for the man whose heart is perfect TOWARD HIM. Peter's reputation was not the best. He was associated in the minds of the people with that denial and cursing at the trial of his Master; but Peter's character was all right; he had wept in penitence and repented of his sin. The relation between him and God

was such that He filled him with his Spirit and used him powerfully.

HINDRANCES.

1. *Sin.*—"If I regard iniquity in my heart, the Lord will not hear me." Ps. 66 : 18.

2. *Satisfaction.*—We are weak, because contented to be weak. The old man, who, after twenty years of labor, thanked God that one soul had been saved through his work, was somewhat to blame. "Woe to them that are at ease in Zion!" The Lord Almighty is present, ready to work through our faith, his Word and a good character; and if he does not work powerfully, it is our fault.

3. *Unbelief.*—Can Omnipotence be resisted? Not by any combination of wicked men or demons. But one thing can limit the Holy One of Israel. Doubt is the water which quenches the fire of the Spirit—is the glass which intercepts the current of his power. Jesus, who had opened the eyes of the blind, walked upon the water, fed the five thousand and raised the dead, stood helpless, the hands of his power shackled by the unbelief of those about him. "Why could not we cast him out?" asked the disciples. "Because of your unbelief," said the Saviour; not because my power is absent, but because the channel through which that power flows has been clogged.

4. *Ignorance.*—"Ye do err, not knowing the Scriptures, nor the power of God," Matt. 22 : 29; and we are the Sadducees of to-day in that respect. We are

not powerful, because we have not in mind and heart the Word, with which the Spirit works. We need, however, more than knowledge of the truth; we need to have God's message. By the close study of the Scriptures, let us learn God's truth; by looking to him in prayer for guidance, let us seek the appropriate truth; and the man who comes before a congregation, not simply with the strength of truth, but, what is more, with the conviction that he is proclaiming God's message, is truly powerful.

5. *Pride and Vanity.*—We are PROUD of what we have—we are VAIN of what we think we have, but are mistaken. We may have learning, a commanding presence, a logical mind, good voice, popularity and be proud of it; and that pride is our weakness. But we should specially guard against spiritual vanity. The fact that God has used us in doing something may not be so complimentary after all, for he can use a worm to thresh a mountain. He takes "the weak things to confound the mighty, and the things that are not to bring to naught the things that are," 1 Cor. 1 : 27; and, if through you he has threshed a mountain, it is only proof that you may be a worm. The tendency in us to crave the praise of men should be watched. "How can ye believe," said Christ, "who receive honor one of another, and seek not the honor which cometh from God only?" John 5 : 44.

6. *False Expectations.*—We expect to feel strong; we desire a consciousness of God's presence; we wish to

shake ourselves Samson-like, and realize that there is might in our sermons, in our manner, in our words. We forget that he "giveth power to the faint, and to them that have no might he increaseth strength;" that God's strength is made perfect in weakness; "When I am weak, then I am strong." The Spirit's work is not to show himself to us. "He shall not speak of himself, but will take the things of mine and show them unto you." His office is to lift up a crucified Christ. He teaches us the lesson of hiding self behind the cross. Now, if it was his plan to show himself, we should always feel his presence; but as he works invisibly, we must simply rest on the promise of God, and whatever be our "liberty" or "unction" expect him to be present.

We mistake when we expect that one blessing will insure another. The disciples were filled on the day of Pentecost for that special work; for another work a few days afterward they were filled again; and for every work there must be a new infilling of the Holy Spirit. Our work is never run by momentum. We are apt to think that, if we give a church or an enterprise a good send-off, it will certainly continue. The power that started it must be applied every day and hour.

HOW TO GAIN THIS POWER.

By God's help let us remove the obstacles just mentioned. Are we living in sin? Turn from it. Are we satisfied with weakness? Beg God for dissatisfaction.

Have we unbelief? "Have faith in God." Are we full of pride or vanity? Seek God's message, and ask him to humble us under his mighty hand. Have we false expectations? Let us expect the power from the right source, and yield our wills and plans to God.

But above all

LET US WAIT UPON GOD IN PRAYER.

In the rush of a busy life we are tempted to dispense with times of secret devotion. "They that wait upon the Lord shall renew their strength; they shall mount up on wings as eagles." Is. 40: 31. Our power is in proportion to our inner isolation from the world. Put a man on a glass stool, and you can fill him with electricity until the sparks will fly from all parts of his body. Place him on the earth, and the current passes off. The current of God's power does not fill us, because we are too close to the earth—its vanities, its pleasures, its ambitions. Some one may call you in modern slang "a religious crank." Be willing to seem a crank. I saw that the steamboat in the storm the other night was moved against wind and wave by turning of a crank. A crank with an engine a hold of it can move things. Some people are so smooth, and straight, and prim, that it seems God cannot get hold of them. The Lord send us men who are willing to be peculiar and distinct—to be "cranks," indeed, so that he may powerfully wield them for his glory.

"Tarry ye in the city of Jerusalem until ye be endued with power from on high." Luke 24: 49. Let us cease to tarry, waiting for the coming of the Spirit. He is here. But tarry much with him in communion.

A man to be strong must eat and breathe. Study and digest the Word. Inhale freely this heavenly atmosphere and you will become mighty. We have heard of the traveler rubbing the frozen comrade amid the snows of Switzerland until his own blood began to circulate, and we tell cold Christians to go out and try to save somebody else; thus they will get warmed up. That may be true; but the great heart of Jesus is a furnace heat that can warm us and fit us for activity; keep close to it in prayer and the study of his Word, and you will go forth "endued with power from on high."

II.

ADDRESS OF WELCOME.

BY BISHOP A. W. WILSON.

A MORE grave and momentous theme for consideration could not be presented than is contained in the subject of this Conference. In the later days of his incarnate life, when it was more than ever needful that his disciples should be provided against possible defect and failure in the ministry committed to them, our Lord kept in their thought and fixed their hope upon the Holy Spirit, the promise of which he had received from the Father. He would take of the things of Christ and show them to them. He was to be the teacher and guide into all truth, and bring to their remembrance all things that the Lord had said. When they should stand before the rulers of this world he would teach them what they should say. They should receive power after that the Holy Spirit should come upon them.

When the Lord's bodily presence was taken from them they waited until "they were all filled with the Holy Ghost" before entering upon their ministry, and at the Spirit's dictation, on the day of Pentecost, they spake in the manifold tongues of earth the wonderful works of God.

From that hour they thought only of the guidance of the Spirit, and gave implicit obedience to his command; and each decisive movement of the church was made under the impulse and at the word of the Holy Ghost. Witness the consecration of the church's property, when Levi in person of Joses, a Levite, gave not the tithe, but the whole, to the service of Christ, and Ananias and Sapphira were smitten to death for having "lied unto the Holy Ghost;" the ministry of Philip to the eunuch of Ethiopia, of Peter to Cornelius; and the separation of Saul and Barnabas for the missionary work to which the Spirit called them. The Acts of the Apostles are but the acts of the Holy Spirit.

Looking at the large place filled by the Spirit and the emphasis laid upon his work, in the utterances of our Lord, and in the early history of the church, it is somewhat surprising that so little stress is laid upon his ministry in these last days. May not much of our weakness and many of our failures be attributed to our ingenious efforts to find substitutes for his personal agency?

We are warned in the terms of the notice of this Conference of the dangers to which the church of God is exposed by neglect of the person and power of the Holy Spirit, and are invited to a prayerful discussion of the third person of the blessed Trinity, and meditation upon his functions in relation to the church, the individual believer and the world. It is intended to be, not merely a theological or speculative discussion, but practical, making prominent the experience of the Spirit's work in all aspects of it. It ought to be a Conference very bountiful in results in individual religious life and in the work of the churches. To these ends let us give our earnest attention and direct our prayers.

III.

THE HOLY SPIRIT THE REVEALER OF CHRIST.

BY GEORGE S. BISHOP, D.D.

WE are living in the Dispensation of the Spirit. What does that mean?

It means that we are living on a higher plane than ever has been occupied before. We gather this—

1. From a comparison *of this Dispensation with others that have preceded it.*

True religion is more widely disseminated in this than it has been in any preceding Dispensation. Not only so, but more people, in proportion to the mass of professors of religion are truly spiritual, and spirituality in these has risen to a higher point than ever before—that is, it has been more intelligent, consistent, ardent, aggressive and victorious. We know, for instance, that proportionally there are more Christians now in the world than there were in the time of the Judges—that they will average better, and that they have a more forceful influence than had the early Hebrew tribes. We know, too, that the same fact bears out in a comparison of later results with those of our Saviour's personal ministry. We know that he has more followers now than he had when he was on earth—that intelligence has reached a higher point than it did, even under his teaching, and that Christian effort has been followed by more surprising and more permanent effects.

2. We know that this Dispensation is an *advance, because God himself is advance*—progress. He never goes backward. God known as Diety, comes to be known as Deity in human flesh, and then this Deity, so brought near to us—seen, touched and handled—is known again, "not after the flesh, but after the Spirit."

3. The same fact is clear *from the structure of Scripture*. The Old Testament is the Lock—Christ is the Key to the lock—then the Holy Ghost is the Hand on the key, without which the mystery of godliness had never been opened. Christ is the Revealer of God, and the Holy Ghost is the Revealer of Christ. "No man can say that Jesus is Jehovah, but by the Holy Ghost." These things go to make evident that we are living on a higher plane of light, responsibility, motive and action—*i.e.*, "in a most signal sense,"—in the realm of the Spirit, and

4. *The whole historic development of man*—looked at in the line of the plan of redemption is clearly enough in this upward direction. The work of God is from matter toward spirit. The child leaves his playthings behind, and comes to despise them. The college student turns his back on the pleasures and games of his boyhood. The professional man has forgotten the rivalries of college life—as narrow as its walls; and the

mellowed and matured philosopher "lives already amid the peace and the power of invisible scenes," and draws from above and beyond him the springs of incentive and action. The same principle holds throughout nature. Time and again our attention is drawn to the fact that there is an invisible world, and that that invisible world bears down upon and overpowers the visible. That Thought and Feeling and Volition are stronger than Substance and Quality and Force, and that from within what is unseen and supersensible and supernatural flow the "upper springs" of all inferior energy and action. That though principles, like Faith and Hope, and Love and Righteousness, like Mind and Heart and Will, are imperceptible, intangible and "hid within the Veil," yet not the smallest work of the obscurest worker nor the grandest enterprise of the most powerful syndicate or Cæsar, but is the effect of their impetus. And so powerfully does this conviction rule mankind that not an individual but at times, and in moral crises, runs back of all second causes and stands subdued and solemnized before such facts as Conscience—Force of Will—an overruling Providence—Remorse—and the straight plummet-line that falls before the Unseen Holiest of all—Eternal Righteousness. All which points upward to the Holy Ghost and emphasizes it that we are living in the Dispensation of the Spirit, and that we are moved, most of all, by *powers above* us, not only, but as never before, by the *power of the Spirit*, and that we must look to be led by the *light*, and vitalized for the great work of God by the GRACE of the Spirit—that—in fine— "like holy John of Patmos, we are to BE"—in this Day of the Lord—*in* the Spirit.

5. But we are not left to gather up an inference from observation, nor speculation, nor from logic. "Our *Saviour* Himself now assures us, that if we believe in him we shall do greater works than even those which HE performed on earth, and that we shall do them *precisely* because he goes to the Father."

This he explains by saying that it is expedient for us that he should *go away*, for unless he does go away the Comforter will not come; but if he shall go he will send him.

"And when he, the Spirit of Truth is come, he will *convince the world* of sin. He will guide *you*—the Church—into all truth. He shall *glorify* Me, *i.e.*, make Me *to* you—*through* you, Glorious. The Holy Ghost will fill the world—through the Church—with a revelation of God, in My Person, such as never has been seen nor known before."

That focalizes our attention on three points.

I. The one essential to salvation is the Revelation of Christ. "He shall glorify ME!"

II. The Holy Ghost alone can reveal him. "HE shall glorify Me."

III. The ulterior and special Object of the Spirit's revelation is God's glory in the face of Jesus Christ. "He shall GLORIFY—make Me glorious!"

I. The one essential to salvation is the revelation of Christ.

How essential this is may be gathered from Reason, from Conscience and from the light of the Scriptures.

From *Reason*. Nowhere, outside the radius of Christianity, is there either holiness or peace. Look at Africa. Look at China. Look at Hindostan. My dear friend, Bishop Fowler, of the Methodist Episcopal Church, who has been traveling, as some of you know, of late in those countries, gave me a description impossible here to repeat, it was so terribly revolting. Even then, he said he had not touched the bottom facts.

He who knows anything of the history of moral light knows that it has followed, as its centre, the planting of the cross of Christ—that just as races have receded from the light of God in the face of our Lord Jesus Christ, so they have sunken to a brutish level, and have died in the distractions of an utter unrest.

But not only Reason, *Conscience* affirms the same truth. Conscience, in every man, says: "You are guilty! You are a sinner! You are condemned! God is holy. He cannot acquit. He must punish!"

Conscience, whatever modern thought may say—however it may strive to cheat us—cries, "Eternal Justice is Eternal Fact, and *God* is just; and How can justice clear the guilty?" and to this cry of conscience is no answer but in Christ and in the sacrifice of Christ.

And these deductions of our reason and our Conscience are confirmed by *Scripture*.

The first thing that confronts us in the Bible, after the record of Creation, is a guilty man, and the whole Book goes on to deal with guilt, not as an accident, but as the one great fact on which are based all other facts of the remedial system.

If there is nothing to be saved from—if there are no parties to be reconciled—if, without reconciliation, there can be pardon, and peace, and comfort, and heaven, then what is our business as ambassadors for Christ and what is the Gospel?

The Gospel is an overture to the LOST—then men are lost. The Gospel is good tidings of SALVATION; then there is a *way* of Salvation. The Gospel is the presentation of a Saviour; then, without that Saviour, men—no matter who they may be—*perish*.

So, the Bible not only represents it, but it *says* so. The first main characteristic of the Gospel is that it affirms.

Every thing else *questions*. Speculation questions. Superstition questions. Higher Criticism—the men who write such books as "Whither" put them always in the form of a question. Infidelity is an interrogation point. The adversaries of the cross of Christ assert nothing, but they question everything. They will not lay down a proposition nor define their opinions. They dare not, for they know that the square, blunt blow of unsophisticated truth will at once demolish their light and fantastic fabrics of falsehood; therefore they skirmish, and cavil, and dodge, and suggest, and propose "certain questions."

Now the Bible affirms. On this point does the Bible affirm? It does. It comes straight out and says: *Apart from the knowledge of Christ there is no Salvation.*

"We are of God, and the whole world lieth in wickedness." "Without the shedding of Blood there is no remission!" "Neither is there Salvation in any other, for there is *none other name* under heaven, given among men, whereby we must be saved." Thus is our first point established—the one essential to Salvation is the revelation of Christ.

II. The Holy Ghost is the only revealer of Christ. He *alone* makes Christ glorious.

The Holy Ghost has given us all the knowledge that we have of Jesus Christ.

Where do we get that knowledge? How do we know that there is such a thing as a Saviour? From the Bible. Outside the covers of this book there is not a hint of a Christ. And whence came the Bible? It was inspired. Who inspired it? God, the Holy Ghost.

Not only so but, with the Bible in our hands, how can we know anything of Christ, save as the Spirit reveals him?

"The letter killeth," says the Apostle. It is so. The letter killed in the Old Testament. Of what avail were miracles? Were all theophanies? Visions of angels? All shocks on the senses?

Of none whatever. Miracle never changed any man. Appearances—like that of the Angels to Abraham—like that of the Burning Bush, or the wheels of Ezekiel, or the Fire that came down on Elijah's altar at Carmel, never changed any man, except as with them, went a supernatural light and voice.

Abraham saw Christ's day. How did he see it? By *illumination*—by the Holy Ghost. Moses recognized God at Horeb. How? By the fire? No, but by God speaking out of the midst of the bush. Ezekiel was transformed at Chebar. How? By the wheels? No, but "*the Spirit*," he says, "entered in me." Israel was to be revived under Elijah. How? By the wind? By the earthquake? By the fire? By any sensible and ocular demonstration? No; but by the still small voice. That was the lesson taught to the prophet.

The same fact comes out in the New Testament. How many saw Christ—touched Christ—said they believed on Christ in the flesh, who never went beyond impressions of their outward senses. We are often tempted to think that if we could have lived when Christ lived we should have found it easier to be Christians. It is a mistake. What makes a Christian is the Spiritual apprehension of Christ, and the Holy Ghost alone can reveal him.

He alone did it in the Old Testament. The Old Testament is full of Christ—as full as the New is. See how, in preaching Christ the apostles quote the Old Testament.

Luther used to say he could tell whether the Church was gaining or losing life-power by the study or neglect of the Hebrew. Why did he say it? Because the study of Hebrew means the Old Testament, and because the Old Testament is the casket which contains Christ. The New Testament is the key to the Old, but when we have a key, we do not turn our backs upon the lock, and laugh away the lock—we open it.

The *Old Testament is full of Christ.* Take the 22d Psalm, where he cries, "My God, my God, why hast thou forsaken me?" Take Isaiah 53: "He was wounded for our transgressions, he was bruised for our iniquities." Take the *Levitical Sacrifices*—How without these could we explain the Atonement?

Yet only a few who read them under the Old Dispensation, saw Christ in these Scriptures and why? Because they needed more than the most perfect description. They needed light on the light. They needed, like David, to have their eyes opened to see wondrous things out of God's law.

They needed, like Simeon and Anna, in the temple, to have something more than had other spectators. Something more than the mere presentation of Christ. Something which should make them take him in their arms and exclaim, "Mine eyes have seen thy salvation!"

The same thing is true *of the New Testament.* It is, of course, full of Christ and nothing but Christ and yet, in the gospels, when Christ himself was living and walking among them, we may say of most, as it is said of the disciples, who were journeying to Emmaus,

"Their eyes were holden that they should not know him."

St. Peter in Matt. 16: 23 responds in answer to the question of Jesus, "Thou art the Christ, the Son of the living God." But how does he say it? He says it, not in his senses, but like a man transfigured, by a fire that burns in him and out of him in a new flash of fact as well as expression—"Blessed art thou, Simon Bar-Jona, for flesh and blood hath not revealed it unto thee; but my Father which is in heaven."

Thomas, in John 20: 28, cries out in a rapture, "My Lord and my God!" He sees and he adores the Deity of Christ. From the most incredulous of the eleven he comes to be their leader, and by appropriating faith to confess and to claim the Lord Jesus as God.

He does this without ever putting Christ to the test that he had laid down for himself. He does it unexpectedly, suddenly.

How often do we lay down tests anticipating how the Lord shall come to us. He must come this way or that way, by a convulsion, by a vision, by some recognized demonstration or else we must refuse credence. "Except I shall put my finger into the print of the nails and thrust my hand into his side, I will not believe."

If you will look back at the chapter, you will find it a blank as to any handling of Jesus, such as Thomas proposed. Instead of this, is a silence—a check. The GODHEAD COMES IN—a more than human majesty clothed—a more than human glory enhaloed the mysterious Person who thus unexpectedly revealed himself to Thomas and repeated, as out of eternity to him, the very thoughts of his heart.

Thomas saw a man before him with a great wound gaping in his side, more than enough to have caused any death. He saw that wound bleeding, yet the man living and speaking—speaking his own words which none could have known beside an omnipresent, invisible Listener, and Thomas cried instinctively, "My Lord and my God!" How did he do it? By *illumination*. Because the Spirit taught him to cry. Because, all at once, in Christ's light, he saw light.

The Holy Ghost reveals Christ. He glorifies Christ. Notice. He does not create Christ; he shows him.

Christ is all the while there. A person is in a dark room. You cannot see the person; you do not know he is there. Then some one brings in a candle and you see the person revealed—touched with all the radiance of the candle, brighter in outline, more distinct and glorious in feature for the very darkness against which he stands.

When we were sailing in the Grecian Archipelago we came, at dawn of day, to the Island of Rhodes. At first we saw only a grey indistinctness—the shapeless outline of vast rocks rising out of the water. Then as the sun came up, how glorious! There lay the harbor once bestridden by the famous Colossus, the sapphire ripplings of the water touched with rose and gold—the ships, the flappings of their sails stirred lightly by the morning breeze. There stretched away the green fields and the mountains round which poetry had thrown her charm; midway in the perspective rose the ancient castellated ramparts of the fortress of the Knights of St. John, all flashing, glowing, burning, touched and "transfigured by the ministry of light." "That which doth make manifest is light." The Holy Ghost is the only revealer of Jesus.

And the Holy Ghost glorifies Christ or reveals him in his true glory now, as he could not possibly do were Christ present.

One thing: it was necessary that Christ should go away in order that the power of a natural, carnal, earthly influence might be broken.

The apostles loved Christ too much, as the carnal loves the carnal. They limited his power as Martha did when she said: "If Thou—meaning his bodily presence—hadst been here, my brother had not died."

That is the error of Rome with her crucifixes, her Mass and her sensuous ecstacies. Read the memoirs of Santa Teresa and of St. John of the Cross, and you will find the love they express for the Saviour is sensuous—carnal. There is something lurid about it. You are afraid of it.

It was necessary that that sort of thing should be broken—that there should come an experience, which, permit me to say it, should *emancipate* Christ—should burst the tomb and the grave-clothes, and set him Infinite, Omnipresent, Omnipotent, Heavenly—working *above*, as ever *in*, and *through* his church—an experience like that of St. Paul when he says: "Yea, though we have known Christ after the flesh, yet now henceforth know we him no more." We only know him as the Spirit reveals him.

You have known a man by his clothes—by his face—now you come to know him by his CHARACTER. Something reveals him in his abilities, in his integrity, in his truth, as your friend. Then, whether he be present or absent, you can say, "I know him. I can count on him now as never before."

The Holy Ghost reveals Christ. But let us come closer; *the ulterior and special object of the Spirit's revelation is God's glory in the face of Jesus Christ.* That is our

III. Point. "He shall glorify"—"Make me GLORIOUS."

St. Paul expands our Saviour's statement in these words: "For God, who commanded the light to shine out of darkness, hath shined in our hearts, to give the light of the knowledge of the glory of God in the face of Jesus Christ."

The Apostle institutes a wondrous parallel with the original creation. Indulge me while I press that parallel in its out-starting facts.

"And God said, 'Let there be light,' and there was light"—a luminous but undefined Aurora like that of Northern climes in winter, when objects are apparent, indeed, but not glorified. Then, on the fourth day the Sun rose on this Earth. What a change! What a glorious transfiguration of the material Earth, when the Sun rose upon it in splendor!

On the fourth day the Sun rose. What a fact! How everything on earth was touched and changed by this! Let us try to conceive the difference between the first three days and the fourth, when the Sun rose in his splendor; and then let us try to take in the stupendousness of the parallel made by St. Paul.

The world without Christ, or Christ in twilight—beneath the dawn-line of the Old Testament—beneath the histories, and types, and prophecies—beneath the horizon of an Arctic winter, and *then,* and all at once, and forever, the Sun of Righteousness in visible perfection of his glory—the Mystery of Godliness—the Dayspring from on high!

"God, who commanded the light to shine out of darkness, hath shined in our hearts"—creation is the prelude and the prophecy of a yet higher and more sublime irradiation—"to give the light of the knowledge of God's glory in the face of Jesus Christ."

The statement of this point, involves, of course, three. That there is such a thing as the knowledge of the glory of God—that this knowledge is unfolded in the face of Jesus Christ, and that it comes by a Divine in-shining.

1. The knowledge of the *glory* of God. If God *be* God, he is *glorious*, for glory is manifested excellence, and God is most excellent, and cannot be hid.

The glory of God is not only his greatness, but *the equipoise of his character*. Satan is great, *i. e.*, in faculties, but he is in no wise glorious, but infamous because of the defect of his character. Michael, the arch-angel, originally no greater than Satan, and perhaps not so great, is more glorious because of the perfection—the balance of his character.

God's glory is the equipoise of his attributes. With him no where is there too much—no where a deficit.

> "A God o'er all consummate, absolute,
> Full-orbed, in his whole world of rays complete."

All heresy starts from the centre, *i. e.*, by unpivoting God, by disturbing the balance of the Divine attributes, by making God lop-sided, by contending for power to the exclusion of rectitude, or for sovereignty, to the exclusion of self-consistency; or for justice, to the exclusion of mercy, or for mercy to the prejudice of justice.

God—unsupported, unsuspended, self-sufficient—is an Orb at rest—*ponderibus Libratus Suis*, equally balanced every way by his own weight. There is no more power in God than there is righteousness, and no more sovereignty than self-restraint.

It is because God is balanced and must balance that he is what he is, and no conscience, however clouded—say or think whatsoever it please—can ever be at peace until it sees Eternal God *himself* at peace. A God one-sided, careened and tilted by the overponderance of any attribute—a God at war with himself, like a sun on fire devoured by mutually contending flames, were an object of horror—fitted only to drive to distraction. Such a God—were it not a mental contradiction to try to conceive him—could never give peace.

It is important to put emphasis upon the fact before us, because the effort of to-day is to destroy the balance of the attributes of God—to posit it that justice, for example—and in measurement, and in adjustment everything comes back to the straight line—that justice in God is a *merely optional attribute.*

"How can God," says one of our modern Neologians,* "How can God *be free* if he be the slave of his own justice?"

As well ask, "How can I be free if I cannot rid myself of my back-bone? I am the slave, then, of my back-bone. But how can I be a man and have no back-bone?"

For God to be free from his justice would be for him to be free from himself as moral, and therefore immoral—for justice is simply looking on things as they are, and treating them accordingly, and to deny this is to deny rectitude, and to deny rectitude is to deny God and make him immoral.

"God is a Spirit, infinite, eternal and unchangeable in His being, Wisdom, Power, Holiness." Holiness consisting, and in that order of "justice, goodness and truth." Not goodness first, as if God were mere law-

* Author of "Whither."

less, reckless good-nature, but justice first—and yet, not justice only, but *equally* goodness, because he *trues*—i.e., is truth.

How can you improve on the told definition? It came to Sir Harry Vane on his knees, while praying for light. Did he not get the light? Outside of the Scripture, what ever has come so near to direct inspiration?

Throw away your Theology—nay, throw away your Bible, and, in the light of common sense alone, how can you make "love"—and by love, of course, is meant *love to lost sinners*—how can you make *that* any more than the old definition has made it without making it unholy, bad and *wicked* love? What sort of a love is that which has been severed from holiness, justice and goodness?

Justice optional! What should we think of a *man* to whom it were optional to be just, or to be unjust?

What should we think of our courts if it were conceded that judges might rule as they pleased—no matter what the evidence—no matter how glaring the facts? The moral grandeur of God is his balance, his poise, that he rights himself. "Shall not the Judge of all the earth do right?"

2. The glory of God then, as it stands revealed in vast concentric haloes, circles upon circles of immeasurable excellence is at its brightest spot—its centre—and when focalized and gathered to one burning point, nothing more, nothing less than CONCILIATION OF JUSTICE AND

GRACE. "How can God be just and justify the guilty?" lies at the root of the Gospel. The answer to that question *is* the Gospel, and Christ on the cross is its sum.

Christ on the *cross,* not Christ in pre-existence, transcending thought as is the mystery of everlasting generation.

Christ on the cross, not Christ incarnate, in the wondrous constitution of his Person—web-work as it is, and master-piece of all the attributes of God combined—as if the sun should come down out of heaven and shine in, and through some creature making it forever a sun-creature.

Not Christ, a babe, in glory streaming from the manger.

Not Christ when twelve years old, the fair Divinity but softly breaking through his youthful form and gesture as he stands questioning the doctors and unveiling the Messiah of the Scriptures in such wise as to anticipate his whole commission and to make rejection of him from that moment, the unpardonable sin.

Not Christ again in all the grand kaleidoscopic aspects of his ministry, as miracles spring up beneath his footsteps like fresh flowers.

Not Christ in any, nor in all, these revelations, glorious as they are, but still subordinate, but Christ upon the tree.

Christ on the cross, his visage marred more than any man's, bore witness to God's truth. It was there the vision of God's glory shone the brightest "in the face of Jesus," stamped with Divinity and stained with blood.

It was there seen that God would not swerve—that sin must be punished. It was also seen that God would punish sin by punishing himself—that the whole united Godhead would suffer—the Father in giving his Son from his bosom—the Son in agonies of blood and death—the Holy Ghost in joint participation of co-equal sufferings, and in the grieving to which he submits—before God would, in any wise, clear the guilty.

Christ on the cross bore our guilt. As a race we lay crushed beneath it. Imagine a weight like that lifted and borne by one helpless Man—a weight that all the Angels, Cherubim and Seraphim and Powers could not have raised by one united and stupendous straining! Yet he raised it, and not only so, he, the mighty Scape-Goat of iniquities, bore it away to a land uninhabited —sought for, it cannot be found.

What is the upshot of this? The upshot is that from the instant you and I look away to Christ as our Substitute; we are eternally saved.

"The guilt of twice ten thousand sins one offering takes away."

> "If Christ has my discharge procured
> And freely in my place endured,
>   The whole of wrath Divine,
> Payment God cannot twice demand,
> First, at my bleeding Surety's hand
>   And then again at mine."

"Therefore, being justified by faith, we have peace with God through our Lord Jesus Christ," not through our moralities, nor feelings, nor ceremonies, but alone and solely through him.

Is not that glorious? Bursts there not a glory from that torn flesh which hangs and writhes upon those ragged nails, which challenges all suns to rival it in splendor?

Is not here God's glory focalized, as it swings low and kisses even your and my horizon? When we were at the North Cape, at midnight, a French gentleman took out a sun-glass and burned a hole in his hat with it. Low as the sun was, he was still clothed with all his burning power.

So is it with our Saviour on the cross. "For though he was crucified through weakness, yet he liveth"—there, yes *there*, he liveth—and for you and me he liveth —"liveth by the power of God."

"For God who commanded the light to shine out of darkness, hath shined in our hearts, to give the light of the knowledge of the glory of God in the face of Jesus Christ."

3d. This glory hath *inshined*—that is the third point. It hath shined not historically—not in the face of a physical Christ, although these, of course, are included; but through the veil on the heart. Christ's glory to mere worldly men is a veiled glory; "the veil," says the apostle, "is upon their heart."

That veil has been rent—not from our side—from God's side. Not from the bottom where *we* could take hold—you and I could not rend any Veil; but from the *top*—where God can take hold—to the bottom. Christ, full length, appears; let down as a Saviour for sinners —let down where we are, at our last and our lowest— let down where we can take hold; and God says, "Take hold! I have rent—I have split down the Veil."

God hath "*shined in*"—not into the world only, that is not enough—could not be, for "the light shineth in darkness, and the darkness comprehendeth it not."

Into believing hearts God hath shined. It is not simply knowledge, but it is the *light* of the knowledge. It is not Church instruction, but heart-work— interior *regeneration*. "When it pleased God," says Paul, "to reveal His Son *within me*, immediately I took no conference with flesh and blood."

How then, do we see the light of the knowledge of the glory of God in the face of Jesus Christ?

One way, by *Faith*. Faith is the great opened eye of the soul. We believe God speaking in His Word. We believe that Jesus is God. We believe, and see it in new light, that *in extremis*, in salvation, highest angel equally with highest man avails not. Only God upon the tree can answer God upon the throne.

Another way—the light shines in is by the *Witness of the Spirit*. What is that witness if not a supernatural spiritual emphasis put on the assurances and promises of God, which makes them true to us without a question?

"The Holy Spirit also testifies unto us," says St. Paul, in Heb. 10 : 15, "Their sins and their iniquities will I remember no more." The Spirit bears with the Word, his assurance, IN on the soul. I have not only heard Christ's doctrine, but I have his voice speaking *within* me.

> "The Spirit answers to the Blood,
> And tells me I am born of God."

Nothing like this to give peace! It comforts now, amid all sins, all tumults, all perplexities, and it will comfort when the head lies on its last pillow, and can turn and look no where else.

A third way Light shines in is by *Consciousness*. Consciousness of breathing goes with breathing. Consciousness of walking goes with walking. Consciousness of life and vigor goes with power. A man full of the Holy Ghost knows what he is full of, and that he is not empty. He knows that his light is not darkness —that his joy is not despair, and that his power is something other and more than physical elation or physical energy.

"Can he not, through some interior eye which we know not, and for which we have no name, pour into us the radiance of his own infinite glory, though he be the king invisible, whom no man hath seen, nor can see?" Can he not manifest himself to the eye of interior consciousness with a distinctness of spiritual presence as satisfying as that which his bodily form gave to the external vision of his disciples? Can he not pour floods on floods of inundating life upon us until lifted, *floated* we shall move like the resistless waves in might of spiritual power?

He can! he *can!* We know it. We have felt it, and the voice of *yearning* irrepressible, has turned it into prayer.

> "Refining Fire! go through my heart,
> Illuminate my soul,
> Scatter thy life in every part,
> And sanctify the whole."

This Revelation of Christ by the Spirit is what the WORLD needs—is dying for—" When he shall come to *you* he shall convince the *world* of sin."

This Revelation of Christ—*fresh* revelation I mean, satisfying our souls, filling, flooding—enlarging us with the light, and the love, and the joy, and the *strength* of the Lord is what we need, my Brethren. What you and I need if we would save a dying world. In other words, we need the Baptism of the Holy Ghost, that we may see Christ and preach Christ.

The reason why we do not get on—have little enlargement—is the lack of this Baptism. And the reason why we lack this Baptism is, that we do not, as we ought, *believe* in it. We look on Pentecost as a stereotype. It stands for us the monument of what was once a living benediction, but is dead. The Holy Ghost is as it were, *mummified* in the Church. He is mechanical, in our conception, latent. He is being carried under our decent ceremonials as the dead emperor Numidian was carried, in his closed litter, into the battle.

Few of us, I fear, are praying as our fathers prayed. "Breathe from the four winds, O BREATH!" in the conviction that the Church's power is the direct impingement of the supernatural—that it is afflatus from on high—or else our gilded congregations are but bleaching bones.

And because we do not *believe* in the Baptism of the Holy Ghost we do not ask for it. We look on men like Whitefield and Carvosso, Brainerd and Edwards, Bramwell and Spurgeon, Cecil and McCheyne as unapproachable examples, and so our sermons drag, and Sunday-school instructions drag, and evangelism drags and life drags.

What we want is A FRESH REVELATION OF CHRIST. As dear McCheyne says, "Christ for me! that's ever new, that's ever glorious." Revivals of religion will begin again, my Brethren, when ministers go back to the A. B. C. of the Gospel—when they consent to crucify their brains and preach upon the simplest texts. "It is a faithful saying." "God so loved the world." The Spirit owns a very simple Christ.

What we want is a FRESH REVELATION OF CHRIST. Not to see him physically, with Huxley, nor intellectually, with the "Higher Criticism" men, but with Bunyan and with Christmas Evans, by the Holy Ghost—

> "To view the Lamb in his *own* light,
> Whom angels dimly see,
> And gaze transported at that sight
> Through all eternity."

"We, beholding as in a glass the glory of the Lord, are changed BY THE SPIRIT from glory to glory." Let us believe this. Let us, too, gaze until WE are changed—our *ministry* transfigured. Until from glory unto glory we anticipate the beatific vision. Then, on our death-beds, if the Lord should tarry, we may say as did the dying John Owen, when there were brought to him the last wet proof-sheets of his immortal Book—"the Glory of Christ"—"some glimpses of it I have had already, but *now* I am going where I shall see it as I have never seen it in this world."

God grant the Revelation *now*, as flesh and blood can bear, and *afterward* the far exceeding and eternal weight of glory for his dear Son's sake.

IV.

"THE ENDUEMENT OF THE SPIRIT."

BY REV. JULIUS E. GRAMMER, D.D.*

"*But ye shall receive power, after that the Holy Ghost is come upon you: and ye shall be witnesses unto me both in Jerusalem, and in all Judea, and in Samaria, and unto the uttermost part of the earth.*"—Acts 1: 8.

THIS was the promise of our Lord to his church. They should receive power from on high. They should be led into all truth. They should have the comforting assurance of his presence and of the Paraclete. The honor put upon the Holy Spirit is so great as to lead us to magnify his office. He is the Lord; and the Giver of Life. The children of God are born of the Spirit, and taught by the Spirit, and led by the Spirit. We see that he is the author of all prophecy, and the witness of Jesus, as the Son of God, by his resurrection from the dead. He is compared to the wind, blowing where it listeth, to show his sovereignty and his freedom. He is likened to the fire, to show his kindling and illumining influence. He is promised to all who ask. Without him the Apostles would have been utterly helpless. It was not by the eloquence of an

* Rector of St. Peter's P. E. Church, Baltimore.

Apollos, nor by the learning of a Paul, nor by the might of worldly force, but by the Spirit of the Lord.

That Holy Spirit of Promise was to be to the church what the Shekinah was to the temple of old; what the breath of Heaven was in the valley of Ezekiel's vision; what the presence and power of Elijah's prayer were to the dead child of the widow of Zarephath.

We see the effect of his presence,

1st. *First of all in the holy boldness it gave the Apostles.* They had been timid and half-hearted. They had fled at the cross, and hid in the upper room. They were weakened by fear of the magistrates and of worldly authority.

Peter denied his Lord, and even the Apostle John forsook him and fled. But what a contrast on the day of Pentecost! See them before the men who had imbrued their hands in our Saviour's blood. That same Apostle tells them they "killed the Prince of life." He bids them "Repent, and be baptized." He is no longer tempted to deny or desert, but he lifts up the standard of the Lord. Surely this is a great contrast. Their courage is more than a match for the most menacing foes. They are not abashed by the scourge of the magistrates, or the dangers of persecution. They appeal to God and are not afraid of men. So it has been in the history of every true prophet endued with the Holy Ghost. See Moses before Pharaoh; Elijah before Ahab. See John the Baptist, with the energy of the Holy Ghost from his birth, and as a great preacher standing before Herod. See Paul before Felix and the world's proudest skeptics. See Chrysostom before Eudoxia, and Basil before Valens; and Luther before the Diet of Worms, and Knox before Mary of Scots, and Cranmer, at the fires of Smithfield. You see how full the Holy Spirit filled the hearts of these brave and devoted men, that they should not fear the face of man. *And surely that is the need of the church to-day.* We shrink from the challenge of giant forms of evil which menace the life of the soul. We need to-day that enduement of boldness which shall teach us to say, "Let no man's heart fail him." Yes, that hopeful courage which shall confront the mountains of defiant evil that they may become a plain before Zerubbabel. Isaiah was "very bold" as he stretched forth his hand all the day long to a gain-saying people.

Surely the want of courage is the want of the Spirit; and when that enduement possesses the soul it can say as did Deborah, "O my soul, thou hast trodden down strength."

"Then were the horsehoofs broken by the means of the prancings, the prancings of their mighty ones." "Greater is he that is in you than he that is in the world."

2d. Again, the enduement of the Spirit taught men to *depend upon the word.* The great instrument of spiritual conquest is the Bible, which is "the sword of the Spirit." "It pleased God by the foolishness of preaching to save them that believe."

St. Paul, writing to Timothy, in the midst of prevailing Gnosticism and error, urges him, "Preach the word, in season and out of season." It is the word which is "the seed." It is the word of God which is quick and powerful, sharper than any two-edged sword. It is mighty through God to the pulling down of the strongholds of sin.

Where the Bible is most read, studied and preached; where its light has shone, there the vital and saving power of Christianity has been most felt. God honors his word. The Scriptures are given by inspiration of the Holy Ghost, and are profitable for instruction in righteousness, that the man of God may be thoroughly furnished unto every good work. Jesus said, "Search the Scriptures." Out of them he taught the disciples and made their hearts burn within them by the way. The great commission is, "Go preach my Gospel." Preach *the word;* not tradition; not speculation; not philosophy or rationalism, not the theories of men.

St. Paul said, "*The Gospel which I delivered to you is the same also that I received,* how Christ died for our sins, *according to the Scriptures*, and that he rose again, *according to the Scriptures*."

You see how our Lord appealed to them, for he said: What saith the Scriptures?" You see how the prophet directs us "to the law and the testimony." A ministry which subordinates the pulpit, dishonors the divinely appointed means of the world's conversion and sanctification.

We are born again of "the incorruptible seed," even the word of God, which liveth and abideth forever. "My word," says God, "shall accomplish that whereunto I send it." And under the influence of that we see the revolutions which have been wrought in society. We see the wilderness changed into a garden and the habitations of cruelty into the abodes of peace.

Surely it is the pulpit which has made Scotland, England and America what they are to-day. It is an open and free Bible which has saved Germany from the condition of Italy, Spain, Austria and South America. It is to a free church, a free conscience, a free education, and above all, to a free Bible—that under God we are to ascribe the present condition of Protestant Christendom. That eminent painter, Kaulbach, has magnificently portrayed the period of the Reformation. As the climax of the thought preceding and growing out of it, he has gathered into a group the representative men of the world before and after that great era. There is Columbus, with his charts, the discoverer of the new world, where the Bible has won its proudest victories. There is Sir Isaac Newton, with his globe and his "Principia;" Sir Isaac Barrow, with his ponderous tomes on the "Pope's Supremacy;" Sir Francis Bacon, with his "Novum Organum;" Dante, the poet of the Reformation, with his "Divina Commedia;" Shakespeare, with his immortal Dramas; Guttenberg, with his printing press, and, in the midst of them all, Martin Luther, with his open Bible lifted to reflect the glory of God, and to shed the beams of the Sun of Righteousness, with healing in his wings. The lesson of such a great painting is clearly this : " The entrance of thy word, O Lord, giveth light—it giveth understanding unto the simple."

"Brethren," says the Apostle, "pray for us, that the word of God may have free course and be glorified."

3d. Again, we see the enduement of the Holy Spirit in keeping the Apostles, and their true successors, *loyal to their commission.*

They preached Christ. In Corinth, with its luxury and rich commerce, St. Paul determined to know nothing but " *Jesus Christ, and him crucified.*" In Athens, with its sculptured monuments and its temples of imposing grandeur, he preached " *Jesus and the resurrection.*" In Ephesus, with its witchcraft and magic, " fear fell on them all, and *the name of the Lord Jesus* was magnified. And many that believed came and confessed and shewed their deeds. Many of them also which used curious arts brought their books together and burned them before all men : and they counted the price of them and found it fifty thousand pieces of silver, so mightily grew the word of God and prevailed."

In Rome, " where," as Tacitus said, " everything vile came," the Apostle says he was not " ashamed of the Gospel of Christ; for it is the power of God unto salvation to every one that believeth ; to the Jew first, and also to the Greek." " Christ first, Christ midst, Christ last," was the theme of Apostolic preaching. It was not ecclesiasticism; it was not ceremonialism; it was not to confront the opposition of " science, falsely so called;" it was not "profane and vain babblings." IT WAS CHRIST. We see this characterized their preaching everywhere. As Philip preached to the treasurer of the queen of Candace, it was "Jesus" and his sacrifice. The Holy Spirit blessed it and the chamberlain "*went on his way rejoicing.*"

"Unto me," says the Apostle, "is this grace given, that I should preach among the Gentiles the unsearchable riches of Christ." Jesus said, "He shall take *of mine* and show it unto you." "He shall glorify *Me.*"

4th. Again we see the enduement of the Spirit *in the exercise of a faith which depended upon the power of God.*

"Who is Paul?" says the Apostle, and "who is Apollos? but ministers by whom ye believed." The sovereignty and grace of the Holy Spirit were not confined to men of learning or eloquence. The humblest witness for Christ might become an instrument of untold good. An Aquila and a Priscilla could teach even an Apollos "the way of the Lord more perfectly." The most obscure servants of Christ have been raised up for his work, to show that the weak things are often chosen to confound the mighty, and "things which are not" to bring "to naught things that are; that no flesh shall glory in his presence." And certainly we have lived to witness that in our time. We have seen an Evangelist, with no equipment of scholarly attainments, with none of the polish and erudition either of the theologian or the cultured orator, moving multitudes and calling them to Christ, as no minister, possibly, of modern times. Can any one doubt that it is "the finger of God;" that it is the power of the Spirit; that it is the power of Elias and John the Baptist and of the Lord himself, illustrating the enduring wealth of his promise, "Cease ye from man." Remember the record which is given in The Acts, "Now when they saw the boldness of Peter and John, and perceived *that they were unlearned and ignorant men*, they marvelled; and they took knowledge of them, that they had been with Jesus."

We emphasize this, not that we would discourage learning, but to *show how God, the Holy Spirit*, uses men of low degree often to do such a work so as to magnify his Grace. We find Peter and John, as well as Paul and Apollos, able ministers of the New Testament; and clothed with a wisdom above the world, yet never having been taught. Certainly we have great reason to rejoice in all the contributions of a profound erudition to the wealth of the Church's literature. We see many great names in the mighty host of stars which Jesus holds in his right hand; but we see among the brightest of them those who were best known, because "They were wise to turn many to righteousness." They were poor, yet made many rich. They had nothing, and yet they possessed all things.

5th. Nor should we forget to notice *the enduement of the Spirit in its world-embracing zeal.*

"They went *everywhere*, preaching the word." No Jewish exclusiveness confined them to the house of Israel. The house of Cornelius was admitted as a sharer in those benefits. St. Peter says, "The promise is unto you, and your children, and to all that are afar off." They saw that the middle wall of partition was broken down. They went "far hence to the Gentiles," and to the utmost bounds of the earth. Not only to Philippi, but to Rome, and not to Rome only, but into all the world. The Spirit of God while it recognizes all distinctions of government and of administrations, secular and sacred, at the same time it teaches us that the whole world is guilty before God, and in need of the common salvation. And while men talk of "Catholicity," let us learn from the Spirit that he is a catholic who loves God and his neighbor, who loves Christ and his Gospel. He is a catholic who learns, under the enduement of the Spirit, to realize that there is neither Jew nor Gentile, Bond nor Free, Greek nor Barbarian, in the light of the Gospel; but all are "One in Christ."

This is the Charity which rejoices in the Truth: which makes Christ Head and teaches that all we are brethren. The whole Spirit of the Gospel is opposed to proselytism. It seeks not to build up party, or sect, or hierarchy, but to add to the followers of Christ. "*He shall glorify Me;*" not schools of thought, not the monuments of the world's wisdom and philosophy; not organizations, or ecclesiastical Shibboleths, but Christ; Christ as Saviour, Teacher, King.

St. Paul said he was "all things to all men" (without the compromise of any principle) "that by all means he might save some." And when we catch that motive and the true meaning of that principle, we have the Spirit of Christ.

The reigning desire of the Church is for unity. And according to the measure, in which we have that love and loyalty to Christ, will we "love all those who love him." Surely there is a volume of truth in that passage of the Apostle, "Some, indeed, preach Christ, even of envy and strife; and some also of good will. The one preach Christ of contention, not sincerely, supposing to add affliction to my bonds. But the other of love, knowing that I am set for the defence of the gospel. What then? notwithstanding, every way, whether in pretence or in truth, Christ is preached; and I therein do rejoice, yea, and will rejoice. For I know that this shall turn to my salvation through your prayer, and the supply of the Spirit of Jesus Christ, According to my earnest expectation and my hope, that in nothing I shall be ashamed, but that with all boldness, as always, so now also Christ shall be magnified in my body, whether it be by life or by death."

What better attainment can we hope, and labor, and pray for *than such a spirit?* The nearer we are to Christ the nearer we are to each other. The nearer to the Head, the more we shall say, as John the Baptist, "He must increase, but I must decrease." "Not I," says the Apostle Paul, "but Christ that dwelleth in me."

If there is any meaning in our coming together, it is that we may have that zeal, which is according to knowledge, that faith which worketh by love, and that love which prays for the peace and prosperity of the City of God. Let our citizenship be as it becometh the gospel of Christ, that we stand fast in one spirit, with one mind striving together for the faith of the Gospel.

V.

THE SPIRIT'S THREEFOLD CONVICTION.

BY GEORGE DANA BOARDMAN, D.D., LL.D.

" *When he is come, he will reprove the world of sin, and of righteousness, and of judgment: of sin, because they believe not on me; of righteousness, because I go to my Father, and ye see me no more; of judgment, because the prince of this world is judged.*"—*John* 16: 8–11.

THIS pregnant paragraph sets forth the three chief offices of the Paraclete in his relations to men in this æon. When he is come, he will convict the world, first, in respect of sin, because they believe not on Christ; in other words, the Spirit is to bring to the world the conviction that there is such a thing as sin, and that sin consists in the refusal to believe on Jesus Christ. The Spirit is to convict the world, secondly, in respect of righteousness, because Jesus has gone to the Father, and we behold him no more; in other words, the Spirit is to bring to the world the conviction that there is such a thing as righteousness, and that righteousness consists in Christ's incarnate career, as demonstrated by his return to heaven. The Spirit is to convict the world, thirdly, in respect of judgment, because the prince of this world hath been judged; in other words, the Spirit is to bring to the world the conviction that there is such a thing as judgment, and that judgment consists in the triumph through Christ of righteousness over sin. In this paragraph, therefore, is compacted an outline of man's guilt, Christ's righteousness and Jesus' final victory over Satan; that is to say, a compendious moral history of the world from the Eden that has been to the Eden that is to be. And now let us ponder the profound paragraph in detail.

I. *The Spirit's Conviction of Sin.*—And first, the Spirit's Conviction of Sin :—" *Of sin, because they believe not on me.*"

1. This is not society's definition of sin: according to society, sin means crime, vice, immorality. Neither is it the philosopher's definition of sin: according to the philosopher, sin means misdirection, abuse, disease. Neither is it the theologian's definition of sin: according to the theologian, sin means transgression of God's law, coming short of God's glory, hereditary guilt. But it is Christ's definition of sin: according to Christ, sin means unbelief on himself, unbelief in Jesus as the Christ and Son and Image and Revealer of the Father. "Of sin, because they believe not on me." And this is sin indeed. For the Word made flesh is Immanuel, God-with-us. To disbelieve on Jesus, then, is to disbelieve on Deity himself. Whosoever denieth the Son, the same hath not the Father (1 John 2: 23). Christlessness in a Christian land is atheism. Sin, therefore, became a new thing when Jesus came into the world. Recall what he himself had just said:

"If I had not come and spoken unto them, they had not had sin: but now they have no excuse for their sin." (John 15: 22.) Therefore it is that disbelief on Christ is the sin of sins, ay, sin itself.

2. Observe now that of this sin of sins the Spirit is the sole convicter. When he is come, he will convict the world in respect of sin, because they believe not on Jesus. And no other power can. The preacher cannot do it; conscience cannot do it; even holy scripture cannot do it. Remember the difference between sins and sin. A jury may convict me of crimes: conscience may convict me of sins. But no power less than the Holy Spirit can convict me of sin. No barb but his can pierce to the root of my nature; no flash but his can show me to myself as a ruined sinner. And the argument he wields in convicting me of sin is this very fact that I do not believe on Jesus. Calvary, not Sinai, is the Spirit's mightiest artillery. Listen to Jehovah's word through his prophet Zechariah:

I will pour upon the house of David,
And upon the inhabitants of Jerusalem,
The spirit of grace and of supplication;
And they shall look unto him whom they have pierced:
And they shall mourn for him, as one mourneth for his only son,
And shall be in bitterness for him, as one that is in bitterness for
    his first-born.   —ZECHARIAH 12: 10.

Thus it was on the day of Pentecost, when Peter, filled with the Holy Spirit, charged on his hearers the crime of the crucifixion so boldly that they were pierced to the heart, and cried, "What shall we do?" And so also it has ever been the experience of every consciously awakened sinner. He feels that John Newton echoes his own experience when he confesses:

> I saw One hanging on a tree,
>   In agony and blood,
> Who fixed his languid eyes on me,
>   As near the cross I stood.
>
> Sure, never till my latest breath,
>   Can I forget that look:
> It seemed to charge me with his death,
>   Though not a word he spoke.
>
> My conscience felt and owned the guilt,
>   And plunged me in despair;
> I saw my sins his blood had spilt,
>   And helped to nail him there.
>   —JOHN NEWTON.

But what avails it to be convicted of sin, unless at the same time we are also convicted that there is somewhere righteousness, and that this righteousness can be made available to ourselves?

II. *The Spirit's Conviction of Righteousness.*—And so we pass, secondly, to the Spirit's conviction of Righteousness: "When he is come, he will convict the world in respect of righteousness, because I go to the Father, and ye behold me no more."

1. "*Of righteousness.*" What is this righteousness of which our Lord here speaks? Whose righteousness is it?

(a) Certainly not the world's. For the world is quite swift enough to detect its own merits. No Holy Spirit does it need to convince it of its own virtues. A very Narcissus it is, seeing everywhere the reflection of its own beauties and worshipping itself. But let us look at this matter a little more deeply, noting what the world's conception of righteousness really is. The clearest and loftiest phase of righteousness among an educated, thinking people will be found, one would suppose, in the object selected as the main purpose or end of life. What then is the object which we Americans set before ourselves as the goal of life? Is it righteousness—clearly and distinctively righteousness? Or is it something less unworldly, to which righteousness is made tributary in way of means to end? Is not success the principal thing which we Americans set before us, the grand motto which we give our children when we send them forth into the world;—success in trade, in politics, in literature, in society? True, we admire and value righteousness. But why do we admire it? Because it is righteousness? Or because, in a civilized, well-ordered community, righteousness is one of the conditions of success? Do we not, practically speaking, secretly feel that Thomas Carlyle has hit the truth when in his "Heroes and Hero-Worship" he virtually tells us, Success is virtue; might makes right? Let righteousness but stand in the way of success, and let the choice lie between the two; and then see which the world will choose. Yes, the world crucified, and, were he to return, would virtually crucify again, the only absolutely righteous One the world has ever seen.

(*b*) Whose then is the righteousness the conviction of which the Spirit is to bring to the world? Evidently Christ's righteousness. The antithesis is manifestly between the world's sin—"In respect of sin, because they believe not on me"—and Christ's righteousness—"In respect of righteousness, because I go to the Father, and ye behold me no more." But what part or element of Christ's righteousness is the righteousness of which he here speaks? Evidently, righteousness in the general, complete sense of the word;—the sum total of all that God requires; the righteousness of a perfect character. In other words, the righteousness of which the Lord here speaks is the righteousness which was incarnated in his own blessed person and career and character and work. And of this righteousness Christ's departure and present invisibility are both the illustration and the proof: "Of righteousness, because I go to the Father, and ye behold me no more."

2. "*Because I go to the Father.*" This going to the Father involves several profound things. First, it involves Christ's own death. We ourselves often speak in a similar way: for example, we speak of a dying saint as one who is going home, and, when the last throe is over, we exclaim, "Home at last!" And why did Jesus Christ die, and so go home? Just because he was righteous, and lived in a world which did not believe on him. His very righteousness crucified him.

Again: This going to the Father involves Christ's resurrection. And why was Jesus Christ raised from the dead? Just because he was righteous: he was declared to be the Son of God with power by his resurrection from the dead (Rom. 1:4). What though his own righteousness had slain him? His own righteousness also raised him. Once more: This going to the Father involves Christ's ascension and heavenly enthronement. And why was Jesus Christ exalted to the right hand of the Majesty on high? Just because he was righteous; his exaltation being the reward of his incarnate obedience. Listen to a classic paragraph, the pivotal word of which is the conjunction "*wherefore:*"—

<blockquote>
Christ Jesus, existing in the form of God, counted not the being on an equality with God a thing to be grasped, but emptied himself, taking the form of a servant, being made in the likeness of men; and being found in fashion as a man, he humbled himself, becoming obedient even unto death, yea, the death of the cross: WHEREFORE also God highly exalted him, and gave unto him the name which is above every name; that in the name of Jesus every knee should bow, of things in heaven and things on earth and things under the earth, and that every tongue should confess that Jesus Christ is Lord, to the glory of God the Father.—*Philippians* 2: 6-11.
</blockquote>

What though Christ's very righteousness had crucified him? Christ's very righteousness also raised him from the dead, and exalted him to the right hand of the Father Almighty. Thus Christ's going to the Father was both a revelation and a demonstration of Christ's righteousness.

3. "*And ye no longer behold me.*" Why did not the

risen Lord remain on earth? Why is he not here now, to be a terror to his foes, a comfort to his friends? We behold him no more in order that we may the better understand what righteousness truly is. For righteousness is not a bulk—so many inches cubic; not a weight—so many pounds avoirdupois. Righteousness is a quality, a character. This is one of the reasons why it was expedient for us that Jesus should go away and the Paraclete come; such an exchange gave us a universal and spiritual Saviour instead of a local and bodily one.

Thomas, because thou hast seen me, thou hast believed: blessed are they that have not seen, and yet have believed.—*John* 20: 29.

In other words, the visible Jesus gives way to the invisible Christ, in order that we may the more easily discern and perfectly appreciate what righteousness truly is: "Of righteousness, because I go to the Father, and ye behold me no more."

4. And of this righteousness the Holy Spirit is the sole convicter: "When he is come, he will convict the world in respect of righteousness." And precisely here it is that the world needs conviction. What its conception of righteousness is we have already seen. It may also be admitted that the world does in a certain sense admire Christ's character. Few eulogies are more eloquent, so far as language goes, than the eulogies which eminent unbelievers have pronounced on the Nazarene. But admiration is one thing: loyalty is

another thing. There is a tremendous difference between æsthetic admiration and practical devotion; between assent to Christ's teaching and consent with Christ's character. And what the world needs is to have such a profound conviction of Christ's personal, conspicuous, distinctive righteousness as to yearn for it, crying, O Jehovah, be thou my righteousness (Jer. 22: 6). And this conviction no power but the Paraclete can effect. Conscience cannot do it: all that conscience can do is to reproach and terrify; conscience brings us no divine pardoner, justifier, redeemer. The Bible cannot do it: all that the Bible can do is to set before us right and wrong, heaven and hell; the Bible plants in our hearts no Lord our Righteousness. The means of grace—Sundays, preaching, sacraments, prayer—cannot do it: all that the means of grace can do is to acquaint us with duty; means of grace do not make us actual sharers in Christ's righteousness. Only one power can do it: it is the promised Paraclete. Listen to St. Paul:—

I give you to understand, that no man speaking in the Spirit of God saith, Jesus is anathema: and no man can say, Jesus is Lord, but in the Holy Spirit.—1 *Cor.* 12: 3.

When Jesus was in the region of Cæsarea Philippi, he asked his disciples, saying:

Who do men say that I the Son of man am? Peter answered and said, Thou art the Christ, the Son of the living God. Jesus answered and said unto him, Blessed art thou, Simon Bar-Jonah: for flesh and blood hath not revealed it unto thee, but my Father who is in heaven.—*Matthew* 16: 13–17.

No; neither civilization, nor education, nor philosophy, nor Sunday-school, nor preaching, nor revival effort, nor Bible, can convict us of righteousness. No power can effect this but the Holy Spirit: "When he is come, he will convict the world concerning righteousness, because I go to the Father, and ye behold me no more."

III. *The Spirit's Conviction of Judgment.*—But what avails it to be convicted of righteousness, unless at the same time we are convicted that righteousness will be victorious? And so we pass, thirdly, to the Spirit's conviction of Judgment: "When he is come, he will convict the world in respect of judgment, because the prince of this world hath been judged."

1. "*The prince of this world.*" If you ask me why Satan was allowed to enter this world and usurp its throne, my only answer is this: I do not know. Here is one of those secret things which belong to Jehovah our God (Deut. 29: 29). Where Holy Scripture is silent, there let me be silent also. Of one thing, however, I am only too sure. Satan *is* the prince of this world. A usurped principality though it is, the principality is nevertheless his. See how he lords it over man's moral nature, as disclosed in the various religions of the world. Look, for example, at the world's idolatries; at its Apis, its Baal, its Dagon, its Mithras, its Siva. Look at the Greek and Roman mythologies:

> "Gay religions full of pomp and gold,
> And devils to adore for deities."—*John Milton.*

Or, to keep within our own land, look at the idolatry of second causes, the worship of antecedent and consequent, the adoration of the powers of nature. What is materialism but a sort of sublimated fetichism? Ay, it is to these and such as these that cultivated Americans shout, "These be thy gods, O Israel, which brought thee up out of the land of Egypt." (Exodus 32: 4). Again: See how Satan lords it over man's psychical nature—over the capacities and affections and desires of men, instigating to all passions of pride and selfishness and ambition and hate and lust. Once more: See how Satan lords it over man's bodily nature, driving his thorns in the flesh to buffet us; bringing disease and pain and death and grave. In fine, look at this world as it actually is; its crimes, frauds, robberies, hates, falsehoods, perfidies, oppressions, cruelties, sensualities, blasphemies; its griefs and woes and deaths: look at all these and similar instigations and works of the devil, and tell me, Is not Satan the prince of this world? Aye,

"The trail of the serpent is over them all."—*Thomas Moore.*

2. But is this to be so always? God be praised, no! for the prince of this world *hath been judged*. To us indeed Christ's judgment of Satan seems to be a process still going on. But this is only because we are finite: for this idea of process, or succession in time, is one of the tokens of human weakness. But to the eye of the Son of God the overthrow of Satan was a single act, and an act already accomplished. In like manner, on the

return of the Seventy, he had exclaimed, "I beheld Satan fallen as lightning from heaven." (Luke 10: 17). To his piercing vision he had already seen Satan falling—a fall sudden, swift, flashing, profound, as the thunderbolt. But how was this judgment on Satan effected?

(a) To answer, first, in a general way: it was effected by the incarnation. To this end was the Son of God manifested, that he might destroy the works of the devil (1 John 3: 8). The incarnation itself was a judgment. Accordingly, Milton, in the burst of a true poet's inspiration, represents the downfall of Satan's empire and the birth of Bethlehem's Babe as simultaneous:

> "From this happy day
> The old dragon, underground,
> In straiter limits bound,
>   Not half so far casts his usurped sway:
> And, wroth to see his kingdom fail,
> Swindges the scaly horror of his folded tail."
>   —*Hymn on the Nativity.*

(b) But to give a more particular answer: Satan was judged by Christ's own death. Accordingly, a few days before, Jesus exclaimed: "The hour is come, that the Son of man should be glorified. . . . Now is the judgment of this world; now shall the prince of this world be cast out: and I, if I be lifted up from the earth, will draw all men unto myself. This he said, signifying by what manner of death he should die" (John 12: 28–33).

Observe the sharp contrasts: On the one hand, the prince of this world; on the other hand, the Son of man: On the one hand, the prince of this world cast out; on the other hand, the Son of man casting him out. Observe, also, the significant notation of time: "The hour is now come; now is the judgment of this world; now shall the prince of the world be cast out." It is as though the Lord had said: "Now is the crisis of this world: in the lifting up of myself on the cross it is about to appear whether this world belongs to Satan or to the Son of man; whether he is its prince or I. We know how the crisis was decided. Messiah's heel, bruised for the moment on Golgotha, in the very fact of its being bruised, crushed eternally the dragon's head (Gen. 3 : 15). And so "crisis" swept into "judgment." The prince of the world was judged; and so condemned. The Son of God, through his own death, brought to nought him who had the power of death, that is, the devil (Hebrews 2 : 14). Henceforth the world changed ownership. There, in the very act of being uplifted from the earth, while as yet his life-blood was ebbing, he despoiled the principalities and the powers, making a show of them openly, triumphing over them, nailing them to his cross (Col. 2 : 14, 15). The prince of this world was judged. And in this act of dying the parable of the Stronger than the strong was fulfilled:

When the strong man, fully armed, guardeth his own court, his goods are in peace; but when a stronger than he shall come upon him, and overcome him, and bind him, he taketh from him his whole armor, wherein he trusted, and divideth his spoils.—*Luke xi. 21-22.*

Thus the vision of Patmos was realized:—

There was war in heaven: Michael and his angels going forth to war with the dragon; and the dragon warred and his angels; and they prevailed not, neither was their place found any more in heaven; and the great dragon was cast down, the old serpent, he that is called the Devil and Satan, the deceiver of the whole world; he was cast down to the earth, and his angels were cast down with him. And I heard a great voice in heaven, saying, Now is come the salvation, and the power, and the kingdom of our God, and the authority of his Christ: for the accuser of our brethren is cast down, who accuseth them before our God day and night. And they overcame because of the blood of the Lamb, and because of the word of their testimony; and they loved not their life even unto death. Therefore rejoice, O heavens, and ye that dwell in them.—*Rev.* 12: 7-12.

Thus the last book of the Bible declares fulfilled the doom which the first book of the Bible pronounced on Satan while yet in Eden:—

I will put enmity between thee and the woman, and between thy seed and her seed; he shall bruise thy head, and thou shalt bruise his heel.—*Genesis* 3: 1-5.

3. And this judgment on Satan is a judgment of which the world needs to be convicted: and this, not merely in way of intellectual apprehension, but, especially and emphatically, in way of moral conviction.

(*a*) Thus each Christian needs this conviction for himself. For he is exposed to a thousand discouragements:

for example, the sense of infirmity, the enigma of delays and disappointments and adversities, the prevalence of iniquity, the enmity of Satan himself. Verily he does not yet see all things subjected to Jesus Christ (Heb. 2: 8). Hence he needs the saving power of hope (Rom. 8: 24). He needs the conviction that Christ's grace within him is omnipotent; that the life in Jesus will not be a failure; that the Christian's victory, if he holds steadfast, is a matter of certainty. It is not enough then, that he has it as a theological article that Satan has been judged: what he needs is to have this fact inwrought as a moral conviction into the depths of his own experience and consciousness. What he needs is to be sealed with the Holy Spirit of promise, which is an earnest of our inheritance unto the redemption of God's own possession, unto the praise of his glory (Eph. 1: 14).

(b) And as each Christian needs this conviction for himself in order to his own salvation and victory, so does the Church of the Lamb need it in order to her own going forth and battling under inspiration of assured triumph. What she needs is the certain conviction that the Church's triumph is a foregone conclusion in the divine mind; that in virtue of her joint-heirship with Jesus Christ (Rom. 8: 17), the appointed heir of all things (Heb. 1 : 3), she will share his sovereignty, even already owning this world by a sort of reversionary right; that the kingdom and dominion and the greatness of the kingdom under the whole heaven shall be given to the people of the saints of the Most High (Daniel 7: 27). What she needs is the absolute conviction that the prince of this world has been judged.

4. But how shall this conviction be wrought? By no power less than the Holy Spirit. When he is come, he will convict the world concerning judgment, because the prince of this world has been judged. Conscience cannot work this conviction: all that conscience can do is to make us aware that we are under Satan's power. Neither can philosophy work this conviction: all that philosophy does is to try to make us believe that there is not, and never has been, any Satan at all; that hell is only the obverse side of heaven, or "heaven seen in a side-light." The philosopher does, indeed, talk of a golden age. But what kind of a golden age is it? An age when all that is now anomalous and discordant and monstrous shall give way to universal law and order and beauty; in brief, when the world shall develop into a Godless paradise, from which Satan and Jesus shall be alike aliens. Whereas the true Golden Age is when the reign of Satan shall be confessedly supplanted by the reign of Jesus; when the whole earth shall become the paradise of his grace ; when his righteousness, permeating all life, spiritual, mental, emotional, corporeal, shall mantle the world from pole to pole, and his infinite beauty girdle it as with a celestial zone. And the conviction that this shall be the final issue can be wrought by no power but the Holy Paraclete. No

man can say, Jesus is Lord, but in the Holy Spirit (1 Cor. 12: 3). Nor are signs wanting that the final rout of the powers of darkness is approaching. In this mustering of the anti-Christian forces under the marshalship of unbelief; in this hurrying to and fro of principalities and powers; in these commingling banners and gleaming spears and trumpet-clangs; in the very fact of this Convention being summoned to ponder the office of the blessed Paraclete; in all this I think we are permitted to read signs that the God of peace shall bruise Satan under our feet shortly (Rom. 16: 20).

Such is the Lord's promise of the Spirit's threefold Conviction.

Review.—In reviewing our paragraph, observe the order of the Spirit's process. The first thing that we sinners need is to be convicted of sin. To whom little is forgiven, the same loveth little (Luke 7: 47). No sense of sin, no conscious need of Saviour. But vain is the Spirit's conviction of sin, unless at the same time he convicts us concerning Christ's righteousness, and that his righteousness may become ours. This, in fact, is a frequent trouble with a convicted sinner. Jesus Christ seems to him a distant, intangible abstraction, a glittering phantom, a veritable *ignis fatuus* receding as he advances. It is needful then that the Spirit should show us to ourselves; it is no less needful that the Spirit should also show to us Jesus Christ. But vain is the Spirit's conviction of righteousness, unless at the same time he convicts us concerning the certain victory of righteousness over sin; the righteousness being in fact the stately bridge whereon we pass from the devil's bondage to the Christian's victory. And to be convicted of these three things—sin, righteousness, judgment—as the Holy Spirit alone shows them to us, is to know the essence of Christianity, nay, to enter into the possession of it. Verily, it was expedient for us that Jesus should go away, that so the Paraclete might come (John 16: 7).

VI.

ADDRESS.

BY REV. M. D. BABCOCK.

ONE of the most conspicuous marks of the believer who has heard and obeyed the words: "Be filled with the Spirit," is the spontaneity of Christian life and service. The indwelling of the Holy Spirit makes the difference between the positive and the negative Christian—between the one able to give and the one who can only receive—between the one bearing much fruit and the one with little else than leaves. There are Christians whose testimony can be extracted from them, but it is a painful, and sometimes perilous operation. There are Christians who cannot help but testify—whose words, whose deeds, whose methods, whose manners tell plainly whose they are and whom they serve. The difference is the indwelling Spirit. We can hardly discern the light of some who profess and call themselves Christians. The very shadow of others has healing and blessing in it.

It is the difference between the disciple in the dark at the world's fire, away from his Master, disowning and disgracing him, and the Apostle filled with the Holy Ghost, following in the Master's footsteps, speaking fearlessly for him, dying, but not denying. It is the difference between Sinai and Calvary; between the whip of conscience and the cords of love; between fear and faith; between reluctance and readiness; between "must I?" and "may I?"

The Christian who claims the promise and realizes the possibility of the Holy Spirit's abiding presence, can prove all this to himself and others. What is it but the fulfillment of Christ's words: "He that believeth on me, as the Scripture hath said, out of his belly *shall flow* rivers of living water?" "But this spake he *of the Spirit* whom they that believe on him should receive."

Receiving the Spirit, welcoming the Spirit, and then what? Spontaneity! "Rivers—living waters—Flowing!" Not wells from which water can be pumped, but springs that flow by their own force and freedom. Not old accumulated stagnant experience, but new life, new love, new testimony, "a new song" every day. Not a Christian who can be goaded into speaking a word for his Lord, but one who loves to speak—who witnesses because he cannot help it—who sings, "'Tis joy, not duty, to speak his beauty;" whose heart keeps overflowing because fed from an unfailing fountain.

"Shall flow!" Spiritual spontaneity. Its finest issue is the Christian's unconscious power—his unrealized influence. Nothing in our life is so subtle, yet so immeasurably potent. It depends utterly on the abiding presence of the Holy Spirit to direct our unplanned words—our unthought deeds; to develop the Christ life within us, and to bring out—we know not how—the likeness of our Lord in us.

Christian art represents Jesus and the holiest of his followers with a circle of light about their heads, like the shining of the face of Moses, though he wist not that it was shining.

So about the person, radiating from the life of the Christian, in whose heart the Spirit abides, there is that unmistakable atmosphere of light—that evident mind of Christ—that divine something we call unconscious Christian influence which undermines the unbeliever's doubts, which confirms his half realized convictions. He cannot account for it, except by acknowledging that this man has been with Jesus.

It is the final test of genuineness—the fragrance of the flower—the flavor of the fruit. It is vital, not artificial—spiritual, not mechanical. It is the product of living,—the aroma, the aureola that tells that here the Spirit of God dwells.

Said a famous English courtier, of who was for a time in the home of Fenelon, "If I stay here longer this man will make a Christian of me in spite of myself." This is the outflow of spiritual life. This is the fulfilled promise—"rivers of living waters." This is the life that men cannot question—the power they cannot escape—the testimony they cannot gainsay. Would you then witness for God even when you did not know you were seen or heard—unconsciously "setting to your seal that God is true?" Would you so live that men and women, yes, and children, will find it easier to do right when you are with them and harder to do wrong when you are with them? Open your heart to the Holy Spirit. Obey the words, "Be filled with the Spirit."

Do you say this is not for me? You are mistaken. It is not the exalted privilege of the exceptional Christian. It is the plain duty of the every-day Christian. It is not a question of natural endowment, but of spiritual enduement; not a question of birth and education, but of willingness, of plain obedience. "Be filled with the Spirit." Are you willing to obey, to say, "Holy Spirit come into my heart—show me everything that is wrong, cast out every idol, possess me wholly, teach me, lead me, use me, as thou wilt?" Are you willing to offer, nay, to *urge* that prayer till it is answered and take the consequences?

VII.

THE SPIRIT OF SONSHIP.

BY W. J. ERDMAN, ASHEVILLE, N. C.

THE characteristic name of the Holy Spirit in three epistles of Paul, is "the Spirit of adoption."

The title of this address is, however, "the Spirit of Sonship," for the word "adoption" in common use does not express the full truth of the Sonship of believers in Christ. The word is found only in Rom. 8: 15, 23; 9: 4; Gal. 4: 5, Eph. 1: 5. It signifies the placing in the state of a *Son*, of one already a *child* in the family; it is a name contrasting the condition of a child who has attained his majority with that of one who is a minor. Christians do not enter twice into the family of God, once by being born again and a second time by adoption understood in its usual sense. "Sonship" relates not to nature, but to legal standing; it comes not through regeneration, but through redemption; for it believers in God in olden time and the disciples of Christ had to wait until the Son of God redeemed them; and then the Spirit of God was poured out at Pentecost, not to make believers Sons, but because they had become Sons through redemption; once though children they were minors, now they became

Sons, and received the Spirit of Sonship. In brief, Sonship, though ever since redemption inseparable from justification, does in the order of salvation succeed justification. In Rom. 5: 1 justification precedes the "grace" of Sonship in 5: 2. The "access" or "introduction" is of the justified into the presence of God as Father; and it is through Christ and by the Spirit. Compare "access" in Rom. 5: 2, Eph. 2: 18, 3: 12. All this truth is obscured by the inconsistent renderings of the Authorized Version, which translates in Eph. 1: 5, "adoption of *children*," and in the other passages "adoption of *sons*." "Children" is not the equivalent of "Sons" in these scriptures.

The importance too of this discrimination is to be magnified because many Christians, by calling themselves only "children of God," remain ignorant of the distinctive high dignity to which they are called and in which they now stand as *Sons* of God.

As a proof of these statements, the following facts may be considered:

I. The gifts and acts of the Holy Spirit were alike in kind before and after the day of Pentecost.

The Spirit was in the world when John the Baptist announced the future baptism. He himself was full of the Spirit. And of old the Spirit was the author of all spiritual life and power, Ps. 143: 10; and gifts of wisdom and government, of teaching and preaching; the working of miracles and the conviction of sinners, Micah 3: 8, all betokened the presence of the Spirit in the old dispensation.

What then was meant by the promise of John and of Jesus?

II. In the heart of the prophetic Scriptures five promises of a future gift of the Holy Spirit are found, and these are repeated in substance and in literal phrase by the Lord Jesus.

1. The Spirit was to be "poured on all flesh," Joel 2: 28-29, Acts 2: 33; 2. To be "poured on all thirsty," Is. 44: 3, John 7: 37-39; 3. To be "poured from on high," Is. 32: 15, Luke 24: 49; that "from on high" contained the whole mystery of a suffering and exalted Messiah, for sin must first be put away, captivity led captive before the Gift could be bestowed; the Chrism of glory could come only from the pierced hands of the glorified Christ; the Rock must first be smitten before the Water could flow; 4. To be "within" believers in a more permanent and interior dwelling, Ezek. 36: 27, John 14: 17, 23; 5. To be "forever" with them; Is. 56: 21, John 14: 16.

In these passages the "pouring," and "on all flesh," and the "from on high" and other phrases are all in significant contrast, and mark a difference between the Old and the New Dispensation.

The unfulfilled context of these predictions also prove the promises themselves await a future and exhaustive fulfilment in the experience of Israel, whom God has not forever cast away. Rom. 11: 1, 2, 12, 15, 25, 26.

III. But it is as the Spirit of Sonship that the Gift

receives the characteristic name. He was to be given more abundantly, "poured;" but specifically unto believers as redeemed Sons of God, unto children who had attained their majority, and as heirs now entitled to receive the inheritance, and who do now receive the Spirit of Sonship as the first fruits and earnest of the inheritance of the Son of God.

It is this marvellous dignity of a Sonship in glory like that of our Lord Jesus, with all its attendant blessings and privileges, service and rewards, sufferings and glories, that imparts to the Pentecostal gift of the Holy Spirit its peculiar character and distinguishes it from all previous bestowments in the old dispensation.

The minors, *i.e.*, the word "children," in Gal. 4: 1–7, are now of full age; the "born ones," the bairns, words significant of nature, kind, kin, in the writings of John, 1: 12–13, I. 3: 1–3, rather than of dignity and office, are now Sons of God; the new name "Father," the Son of God, came to declare, John 17: 26, was now made known in inseparable association with the new name "brethren," John 20: 17, and the inspired interval of silence between Ps. 22: 21 and the remaining part, in which interval came the death, burial and resurrection of Jesus, is now broken by the rapturous greeting of "the first-born of many brethren," Rom. 8: 29. "Go to my brethren and say unto them I ascend unto my Father and your Father, and to my God and your God." John 20: 17. Not before redemption had been accomplished and confirmed by resurrection could Jesus call his disciples "Brethren," and not until the Spirit of Sonship had been given could they say "Blessed be the God and Father of our Lord Jesus Christ."

The mighty Breath of Pentecost symbolized by the breathing of Jesus upon his disciples on the evening of his resurrection foretold their service not as servants merely, but as Sons.

The *pouring* of the One Gift was not only for acts of service (and acts imply "power") but also for "renewing," Titus 3: 5–6; (the pouring on Paul and Titus was not at Pentecost, yet the same word poured is used, so pointing back to Pentecost as the time when the Spirit was given once for all to dwell with the Church); the Spirit was evermore to deepen and develop their spiritual life and nature as children and Sons, to manifest the life eternal as light and love, the life of the Father and the Son lived and developed in this relationship of Sons of God, and also to equip them for ministry with manifold gifts.

To each He was given for life eternal; and all as one Body, as one Son (Galat. 3: 28; "Ye are all one *Son* in Christ Jesus;" see 3: 26 also where "children" should be translated Sons), were baptized by the One Spirit, and so incorporated as "The Christ," 1 Cor. 12: 12–13, "the Son of God, the perfect Man," Eph. 4: 12–13, the Heir, Gal. 3: 16, 19, the Seed, the Isaac, Rom. 4: 16–25, the risen *from* the dead, Rom. 1: 4, Philip. 3: 11, Luke 20: 34–36.

IV. The Spirit as uniting believers with the risen and glorified Son of God works in these three departments of Christian life and experience; the work of faith and labor of love and patience of hope in our Lord Jesus Christ. 1 Th. 1: 3.

"The work of faith" pertains to the realization and experience of salvation and its fruits in all holy virtues and excellencies, Phil. 2: 12, 1: 9–11, but it is wrought out only by faith and the indwelling Spirit of the Son of God, "I in you," John 17: 26, Gal. 2: 20.

"The labor of love" pertains to all service and toil of ministry to fellow believers and to the world, but it is done by the indwelling Spirit of him who is the Vine, and said "I will do it." John 15: 7, 14: 13.

"The patience of hope" pertains to all the sufferings, trials and persecutions endured by believers in patient waiting for the Son of God from heaven, 1 Th. 1: 10, 2: 12, 2. Th. 1: 5–10, and the consummation of Sonship in the redemption of the body, Rom. 8: 23, 19; but the patience is to become a joy, 1 Pet. 5: 11, because the sufferings are really those of the Head through the Body; "Why persecutest thou *Me?*" Acts 9: 4–5.

Jesus is indeed the Word, the Verbum, the Verb of life, service and suffering; the to Be, to Do, to Suffer and infinite in all.

Too much has "the Church," "the Body of Christ," lost this consciousness of oneness with the Son of God in glory; too little have Christian life and service and suffering felt the power and comfort of the mighty, quickening Spirit of God; may this great truth of what we are as Sons of God once again become a vivid reality to us and in us, through the indwelling Spirit of Christ.

VIII.

THE HEAVENLY UNCTION.

BY L. W. B. MUNHALL, D.D.

THE word "Unction" occurs but once in the authorized version, 1 John 2: 20. It is from the same Greek word that is rendered "Anointing" in the 20th verse of the same chapter, *Chrisma*. It does not occur in the Revised Version, but is rendered anointing uniformly.

The word anoint usually means "To smear." Here, however, "Unction" or "Anointing" means "Rubbing in." It is the same when Jesus is spoken of as Anointed for his work and ministry. "The Spirit of the Lord is upon me, because he anointed me to preach good tidings to the poor," etc. (Luke 4: 18). "For of a truth in this city against thy holy servant Jesus, whom thou didst anoint," etc. (Acts 4: 27). "Therefore, God, thy God, hath anointed thee," etc. (Heb. 1: 9). The word rendered "Anointed" and "Didst anoint" in those passages is *Chriō*, which signifies "To rub." It is the same where Paul said, "Now he that stablisheth us with you in Christ, and anointed us, is God" (2 Cor. 1: 21).

Jesus said, "When he is come he will guide you into

all truth;" and, "Ye shall receive power (Dunamis) when the Holy Spirit is come upon you;" and, "But tarry ye in the city until ye be clothed with power (Dunamis) from on high.

On the Day of Pentecost the Holy Spirit clothed the Disciples with power, and imparted unto them knowledge, so that they were qualified to proclaim Jesus and the resurrection with ability and boldness. What they received at that time was "Rubbed in."

To what shall we liken these things by way of contrast? Enduement, is like unto ripening fruit. Unction, the mellowing process by which the ripe fruit is made luscious.

Enduement gave them knowledge and courage. Unction, gentleness, patience, meekness, goodness—all the graces of the Spirit, so that, while like their Master, they spake the word with authority and boldness, they were also like him in temper and spirit—loving, sympathetic and of a very great compassion.

Since Christ received the "Heavenly Unction," and the Disciples were not qualified for service and testimony until they were likewise furnished, how ever can we expect to accomplish anything to the glory and praise of him who bought us, without like furnishing.

Let us see what is the teaching of the Word. First, John 6: 63 and 15: 5 teach that man is incapable of doing anything acceptable unto God of himself. "Nothing" is the word used in both passages to indicate the utter inability of the natural man to quicken or bear fruit.

Second, Eph. 2:10 and Phil. 2:12, 13, teach that God has, nevertheless, chosen man as the Agent through and by whom he accomplishes his purposes in grace. An evolution is here taught. Also an involution. God works in and then we are to work out. This is the true evolution. Only God can make something out of nothing. "But we have this treasure in earthen vessels, that the excellency of the power may be of God and not of us."

Third. Is this Anointing for Disciples now? is it for us? In Luke 24:49 it is denominated "The promise of my Father," and the Disciples were commanded to "Tarry in the city, until ye be clothed with power from on high." This promise was made good to them on the Day of Pentecost, and we all know what marvelous results followed.

But some say that this "Promise of my Father" was only for that company in that "Jerusalem chamber." But, in Acts 10:45, 46 and 11:15 we learn that eight years later it was made good to the infant Gentile Church in Cæsarea, in the house of Cornelius, and was attended with similar signs and wonders. The same was also true in the experience of the infant Church of Ephesus twenty-two years later, as seen in Acts 19:6. In John 7:38, 39 we find that Jesus said, "In the last day, that great day of the feast," "He that believeth on me, as the Scripture hath said, out of his belly shall flow rivers of living water, but this spake he of the Spirit whom they that believed on him should receive." "*He* that believeth on me." As certainly for one Disciple as another. "But this spake he of the Spirit whom *they* that believed on him should receive." As truly for us as for the Disciples in Jerusalem, Cæsarea and Ephesus. If they who waited upon his ministry and were personally associated with him in his work, and witnessed his "many mighty works," were not qualified for the service and work to which they were sent, until they received the "Heavenly Unction;" aye, if he himself must needs be anointed to his ministry, how ever can we, who at the best are "nothing," hope to accomplish anything in his service without like enduement? Unless this "Promise of my Father" is also for us, we go to war at our own charges, and our efforts are but the energy of the flesh.

But the "Promise of my Father," in part fulfilled on the Day of Pentecost, is found in Joel 2: 28, 29. Peter quoted it to those who mocked, and declared that the signs and wonders they saw were in fulfillment of this Scripture. That promise was only fulfilled in part on the Day of Pentecost. It reaches on to the times of this dispensation, as the context clearly shows. But it is to be noticed that the Spirit is to be poured out "upon all flesh." That "sons and daughters," "old men" and "young men," "servants and . . . handmaids" are the subjects of his enduement. Surely, therefore, this Unction is for all. "For we are God's fellow-workers."

Fourth. How may we, the Disciples of Jesus, receive the Anointing? In 2 Kings 2: 1-15, we have the story of the translation of Elijah and the spiritual anointing of Elisha. It will serve to illustrate the lesson of this hour to us. Elijah was a type of Christ. Elisha in many ways typified Disciples. Elijah was about to be translated. Elisha knew it. He had a definite desire. Before it could be realized he must be tested. If we have a definite desire for the anointing, that is surely promised us, and without which we can do nothing, we shall first be tested. Christ met us at Gilgal and justified us from our sins, rolled away our reproach. This is what he did at the other Gilgal for poor Israel. Gilgal means circle. Many converted ones are lodged at Gilgal, and we can all stay there if we so elect. Their thoughts and testimony all circle around the hour and fact of their conversion to God. They make no progress in spiritual things, and, of course, never touch the secret of God's power with men. If we elect to tarry at Gilgal we are at liberty to do so. But I trust that, like Elisha, we will press onward. And so we come to Bethel. Bethel means "House of God." Jacob fleeing from his wronged brother's presence stopped here for a night, and God opened heaven to him in a vision. There are many Disciples resting and dreaming at Bethel. They say, " Are you not saved? Have you not mansions in heaven awaiting you?

> 'Come, let us
> Sit, and sing ourselves away
> To everlasting bliss.'"

In testimony meetings they tell of their conversion and then grow eloquent in their descriptions of the heavenly mansions. We may stop here if we so elect, and engage in like contemplation. Let us press on down to Jericho. Jericho was the City of "Palm Trees." It lay in the low, hot, dusty plain of the Jordan, about 850 feet below the level of the sea. The umbrageous palm invited the hot, weary, foot-worn traveler to rest. Why not tarry here? Many have yielded. They are they who spend their time time chiefly in telling of their attainments,—how they have the "rest of faith"—have no fret or worry, but undisturbed repose, and appear to have little or no concern for the multitudes who are hurrying down to death. They will leave a soul-saving work for a testimony meeting, where they talk of their attainments, and give vent to their censoriousness by criticising those who are not willing to loiter with them under the Palms, and who will not pronounce their shibboleth. Such are not truly sanctified. In order that we may be sanctified, truly and personally, it is necessary to get beyond Jordan. So with God's help we press onward to the dark river. Jordan means death and judgment. Jesus "died for our sins," he was judged for us—" He suffered for sins, the just, for the unjust." The dark surging billows rolled over him. Will we pass beyond? We are to reckon ourselves "to be dead indeed unto sin" (Rom. 6:11). We are to believe on him. "For Christ is the end of the law for righteousness to every one that believeth" (Rom. 10:4), that judgment may be passed by us. And so we take our place, separated from all entangling alliances, unto God, and then we are in a position to ask for the fulfilment of the "Promise of my Father." Oh, that, as thus separated, we may "ask without wavering!"

Elisha saw Elijah caught up into heaven. The Disciples saw Jesus taken up into Heaven. We are to look in the same direction. It is the living Christ that has power and authority. What is the matter with the Roman Catholic Church? She has a dead Christ, and consequently is in much darkness and superstition. Every cross and wayside shrine; every horrible *pieta;* every painting of Christ, of any note, almost, in Catholic countries; every sign of the cross—these all tell of a dead Christ. The darkest picture this world ever looked upon was Golgotha's tragic cross. The heavens robed themselves in midnight mourning and bowed themselves to the earth and wept. The rocks, in their dumb grief, burst in sunder because their Creator was put to death by the cruel hands of those whom he came to save and bless. If there were nothing more than this,—if the seal that was placed upon the tomb of Joseph of Arimathea had remained unbroken we would be without hope—death would be to us an unbroken sleep. The cross, self-considered, possesses no potentiality whatever to save and deliver—for "If Christ be not risen, then is our preaching vain, and your faith is also vain. Yea, and we are found false witnesses of God; . . . ye are yet in your sins. Then they which are fallen asleep in Christ are perished" (1 Cor. 15: 14–18). But when we view this darkest picture in the glowing background splendors of his resurrection from the dead, it glows with life, light and beauty. Paul said, "It pleased God, who separated me from my mother's womb, and called me by his grace, to reveal his Son in me" (Gal. 1: 15, 16). The Anointing of the Holy One, is the revelation of the living Christ in the heart and life of the believer by the Holy Spirit. When a Disciple yields himself utterly to God—separates himself wholly from the world, so that he can truthfully say, "The world is crucified unto me, and I unto the world," and thus takes his true place, according to the standing God gives him in Christ Jesus; and, then with unquestioning faith looks away to the living, mediating Christ, and asks the Father, in Jesus' name, to make good his promise, it will most surely be granted.

We all rejoice in the tens of thousands of Church organizations in the world; for their educated and eloquent Pastors; for their millions of members, with their culture, social influence and vast wealth; for the vast machinery of these Churches—their multiplied and ever-increasing agencies and ministries of good; and all their great power. But, all of these and this cannot convict or convert a single sinner. God has written all over everything that is possible to human strength the word Nothing. All these agencies can be used of God to the accomplishing of his purposes of grace, but he alone can give life and power and blessing. Let us be careful that we don't have "Confidence in the flesh"—making the agencies, means and that which otherwise is possible to us, humanly speaking, the end, rather than which God has ordained to an end; and anointed by him, and having all confidence in him, we can go forward from "Conquering and to conquer"—one chasing "A thousand and two putting ten thousand to flight;" "Mighty through God to the pulling down of strongholds."

IX.

GRIEVING, TEMPTING, RESISTING THE SPIRIT.

BY JAMES MORROW, D.D.
Secretary of Pennsylvania Bible Society.

BY this theme we are brought into practical aspects of the Christian life. Elsewhere we have been taught what the Holy Spirit does to us; here we consider what we may do to him.

The terms "Grieving, Tempting, Resisting," although not synonymous, mutually involve or touch each other. Nice distinctions are not here attempted.

Let it be noted thoughtfully that the Holy Spirit *may be* grieved, tempted, resisted. This proves at once his personality and his capability of grief, with our capacity for grieving him.

If this were not a Bible commonplace—"familiar in our mouths as household words"—it would startle us to-day as a very remarkable utterance. To find out the full wealth of this familiar teaching we must restore it to its original lustre. As scholars, with the feather of their pen, brush away the dust from long buried monuments, let us sweep away the dust from our old, perhaps dead beliefs on this subject.

That the Holy Spirit may be grieved, tempted, re-

GRIEVING, TEMPTING, RESISTING THE SPIRIT. 87

sisted by us is a remarkable truth, because it is so unlike the ordinary opinion of men regarding him. If they think of him at all, it is of One apart from the world in which they dwell and remote from the world within their own thinking minds or throbbing hearts. Yet he works on the souls of men—all men—by a most potent influence. They may not be conscious of his action, nor distinguish clearly his enlightenment—warning or judging, approving or condemning—from the voice of conscience or the judgment of pure reason. Yet he occupies his place within "Man—soul," and performs his peculiar work. There is a parallelism to this in the natural world. We know electricity rather from its effects than from its nature. The ebb and flow of tides reveal the influence of the moon without telling us the "why" and "wherefore" of its law. So is it in the world of mind and the action of the Holy Spirit. We know the result called salvation, and trace it truthfully to the energizing cause, when we ascribe it to the Holy Spirit.

Doubtless in this great work there is concurrent action between the soul of man and the Spirit of God. He strove with the man, and the man yielded. He convinced the sinner of his guilt, and the penitent one from ruin's brink cried, "Lord Jesus, save." He took of the things of Christ, and showed them to the soul ready to die—as Moses lifted up the serpent in the wilderness—and when the trusting heart appropriated the infinite merits of the Lord Jesus it was the Holy

Spirit that hastened with the assurance of pardon and inspired the rejoicing believer to sing—

> My God is reconciled,
>   His pardoning voice I hear,
> He owns me for his child,
>   I can no longer fear.
> With confidence I now draw nigh,
> And Father, Abba Father, cry.

It is needful to remember, in proclaiming the necessity of the Spirit's work, the related truth of the dependence and activity of the soul of man. As in the days when the Lord Jesus spake to the fishermen of Galilee and said, "Follow me"—and they left all and followed him; so now, when the Spirit of Jesus says "Come," the docile believer gladly obeys.

In the Kingdom of grace under which we live the Holy Spirit is the Administrator of Redemption. In his administration he uses the Scriptures. Inspired by himself he employs these, both for the conviction of the sinner and the sanctification of the saint. The Scriptures are truth. As such it might be supposed that they would win the approval and accomplish the salvation of man as other truth makes its way into human minds; changing beliefs, forming opinions, creating convictions or widening the mental horizon. But this is not the case.

Teachers of mathematics rely solely and properly on the adaptation of their truth to the minds of the students and depend upon the unaided powers of the mind to accept and act upon such truth. They are right, and they have their reward. But teachers of Christianity encounter difficulties and obstacles in human nature utterly unknown to teachers of other truth. Not merely ignorance, but pride, self-righteousness, prejudice, unconcern, and even hatred of the truth meet the preacher of the gospel at the threshold of every human heart. Although he knows that the truth, as it is in Jesus, is certain as that of the multiplication table, and that it is adapted to the universal needs of humanity, as the key is fitted to the lock, still his only hope of success is in the Holy Spirit. For he alone can snap the withes of pride, prejudice and hatred, which mathematical truth does not encounter. He creates the hunger and then supplies the food. He brings the news of salvation in the words of Scripture to the mind, and also operates upon and within the mind. He takes the Bible truth, and with that conveys the grace necessary to its reception.

When men are not obedient to their heavenly calling the Spirit is grieved, tempted or resisted. He is grieved when they resist his pleadings. He would flood their souls with ineffable light, but they love darkness rather than light. He would fire their hearts with a divine enthusiasm, but they quench that heavenly flame. Then their perceptions of truth and duty become blunted and their affections, towards God and man, benumbed.

Thus to resist God, reveals a tremendous force in human nature. But responsibility hinges here and the dread fact must be stated. The Holy Spirit is sovereign and free in his gracious influences and we are free to follow or to fail, to yield or to resist, to hearken or to harden, to fan the flame of gracious desire or to quench the fire of holy love.

When we are asked how men may grieve or tempt or resist the Spirit, the answer is clear and Biblical.

I. BY DENYING HIS PERSONALITY AND DISHONORING HIS OFFICES.

We ought, as a convention and as churches, to be jealous for the Personality and Divinity of the Holy Ghost. The doubters and deniers are outspoken and blatant. While we are meeting in Baltimore the Unitarians are assembled in Philadelphia. Listening to them concerning Jesus, we can but wail out, with Mary of Magdala, "They have taken away my Lord and I know not where they have laid him." While we proclaim the Personality and Divinity of the Spirit they seem to be in the state of those who said, "We have not so much as heard if there be any Holy Ghost." Doubt is in the air and gathering like a thunder cloud it makes itself heard. When unbelief conspires men of faith must combine. Let us send forth from this Convention a trumpet blast, loud and clear, on this cardinal doctrine of our holy religion and of the word of God.*

* It was in answer to this appeal that the resolution was passed at the closing session of the Convention. Many disciples simultaneously felt the point and propriety of such witness bearing. May he who is thus honored accept the devout tribute to his Person and his Work.

The Scriptures proclaim and we, believe, that the Holy Spirit is not the mere personification of a divine attribute, but the Third Person of the ever blessed Trinity. To deny that is to grieve him.

As the Administrator of redemption he takes the place that the Lord Jesus himself occupied during his earthly life. The departure of the Christ was the condition of the Spirit's advent. Jesus said, "I will pray the Father and he shall give you another Comforter that he may abide with you forever," (John 14: 16). "Comforter"—$παράκλητος$, *i.e.*, one called to the side of another, a helper, as an attorney to his client. Jesus, the first Comforter, is thus succeeded by the Holy Spirit. What Jesus was to those who followed him over the acres "of Immanuel's Land," the Holy Spirit is to all those who should hereafter believe on his name. Did Jesus convince men of sin? So does now the Holy Spirit. To deny that is to resist him. Did Jesus guide men in their quest of truth? So does the Holy Spirit, all who in later days search for it as for hid treasure. There is no tablet like a loving memory and no chrouicler like the Holy Ghost. He brought all things to the recollection of the first disciples and he is with the followers of Jesus still. To deny that is to grieve him. Did Jesus say to a poor sufferer, whose name we shall never know, "Son, thy sins be forgiven thee?" So does the Holy Spirit now to those who conscious of their need take Jesus as their Saviour. To deny that is to tempt him.

Further, let us not forget that Jesus said that the other Comforter was to abide with us *forever*. He has not been withdrawn from his church. We need not pray for his coming as if he had departed. Let us rather ask for manifestations of his presence and power, believing that he is near and able and willing to fulfil his promise to fill us and seal us and guide us into all truth.

Closer still to the heart of Scripture on this great theme, let us examine Ephesians 4: 25-30, for an epitome of sins in the practical life, and where we have the key-note of this address. Please turn to your Bibles and read—and long after these days of holy convocation are over, read the words again. They are the Holy Ghost's. "Wherefore putting away lying, speak every man truth with his neighbor, for we are members one of another. Be ye angry and sin not, let not the sun go down upon your wrath. Neither give place to the devil. Let him that stole steal no more: but rather let him labor working with his hands the thing which is good, that he may have to give to him that needeth. Let no corrupt communication proceed out of your mouth, but that which is good to the use of edifying that it may minister grace unto the hearers. And grieve not the Holy Spirit of God whereby ye are sealed unto the day of redemption."

Look at these sins one by one:

1. *Falsehood.* To speak the truth is due to all men, as well as to God, but here it is urged as necessary to

the perfect brotherhood within the circle of the church. Wilful misstatements, polite lies, half truths, which are ever the blackest of lies—all these are breaches upon mutual confidence among believers. They are more; they grieve the Holy Spirit of God. All paltering with truth in a double sensé, that keeps the word of promise to the ear, but breaks it to the hope, is an offence in Heaven.

2. *Wrath.* The text quoted shows us that there is a possible anger without sin. The flashing out of the pure and liberty-loving soul against cruelty, lies and foulness, is just and right and Christian. Such resentment against evil is needful in our resistance of it. But anger to be righteous must be brief. As the corruption of the best is the worst, so justifiable indignation, when brooded over or "nursed to be kept warm," becomes an injury to the soul. It acts like acid on steel—it stains the white radiance, it mars the placid surface. Then the Spirit is grieved, for such a one gives place to the devil, who finds an opportunity when and where we least expect him—as Bunyan, in the allegory, tells of a by-path to hell hard by the gate of heaven.

3. *Stealing.* This warning against a crime seems out of place in an address to believers. Perhaps it is spoken of, that its counterpart in self-sacrifice might be enforced. Stealing is not here shown to be a wrong committed against society—that goes without saying— but because it is opposed to the proper treatment of our brothers in Christ. It saps the foundations of the per-

fect home life—whether it be the robbing of property or the filching of reputation. Beware of the latter in the church of God. It grieves the Spirit for it wrongs and injures those for whom Christ died.

3. "*Corrupt speech*" (Revised Version). The word σαπρὸς translated corrupt means *rotten*. This is the only place in the New Testament where it is used metaphorically. In Eph. 5:4 it is described at length as "Filthiness" or the talking without necessity of foul and evil things. In studying medicine or even literature professionally, one must learn everything about everything, however malodorous. But to speak of such things unnecessarily, "Dabbling a shameless hand with shameful jest," shows the prurient taste and grieves the pure and Holy Spirit.

"Foolish talking," the talking of fools, *i.e.*, the wicked. This is the Bible meaning of the word and must not be understood as referring to the babbling of imbeciles or idiots. It is God who describes the man as a fool, who says in his heart, "There is no God." We are to avoid the speech of those who, in the name of science falsely so called, would banish God from the universe he has made as well as the speech of those who in profanity or oath, take the name of God in vain. All such speech is corrupt and grieves the Holy Spirit.

"*Jesting*." Perhaps this is the form of corrupt speech to which many amongst ourselves are most prone. It may be the polished wit, neither gross nor vulgar, which spares nothing, however sacred, that may raise the vacant laugh. It seizes upon Holy Scripture as fitting game for ribaldry or pun. It is not guilty perhaps of the *double entendre* that pales the cheek of an innocent girl, and it abjures the coarse, simply because it lacks elegance. But nevertheless it cuts deep into the purity and peace of the soul and it makes impossible all profit from Scriptures that have been travestied. Never jest with the Bible or the spiritual meaning will be lost to you forever.

"Don't quote the Bible to me," said a dying man recently. "I have linked every part of it with a jest and *that* I cannot forget."

. Oh, the sins of speech of which we have been guilty! The desire to shine in conversation, to be entertaining to friends, to avoid the dullness seen in others, these have hurried, even good men, into ignoble levity or impiety. Let us here to-day, brethren, vow not *to do it and not to listen to it.*

Palsy hurts ourselves, and diphtheria is dangerous to the community, but impure speech injures alike speaker and hearer.

For such conduct and for the habits of mind from which it springs we are responsible. Levity over sacred things grows on what it feeds, and grieves the Spirit of God. Cavilling at Bible teaching, through intellectual pride, engenders self-will and prevents the progress won only by devout docility, and thus the Spirit of God is resisted. Then this light grows dim and the altar fires burn low.

Can we know within ourselves when the Spirit is grieved? Certainly. The signs of the backslider appear and "the consolations of God are small."

Prayer becomes Formal.—Private devotions are feeble; family worship is cold or altogether disused. Look at the heap of ashes, white and dead, on the hearth of many Christian homes. They are the burnt-out relics of a once living altar fire, and tell their sad story of the decay of faith. The heathen priest defended his having an idol in his house, as well as in the temple, because he lived there chiefly and needed the presence of the protector. So do we, and we may know the Spirit is tempted when we rely on occasional services in the sanctuary and disregard the quiet hours of devotion at home.

The Bible is Neglected.—The Holy Spirit inspired the book, and he that allows it to become dust-covered on a remote shelf has the evidence in himself of the Spirit's grief and of his own deterioration. For this grief it must be remembered does not arise so much from the offence against himself as from the wrong and injury to ourselves. It mars his plan for our sanctification. As the loving wife or mother grieves over the moral decline of son or husband through strong drink, the sin of youth, or avarice, the sin of age, so the Holy Spirit mourns over man's loss of purity and power. The fine promise of spring is unfulfilled in autumn. Profession ends in failure. Slowly but surely the blight falls.

> It is the little rift within the lute
> That by and by will make the music mute;
> Or little pitted speck in garnered fruit
> That, rotting inward, slowly moulders all.

The fish in the Mammoth Cave are a sad sight—eyeless, for they are in a world of darkness—but immeasurably sadder are human souls that are blind in a world of light—self-blinded, for they have quenched the fire and the light of life within their own immortal natures by neglect of duties, or through worldliness and God-forgetfulness.

There is an evident evil among believers that must grieve the Spirit, even although they may desire to honor him, *in limiting his operations to one course or method.* Many of God's children, like Col. Gardiner, can tell the day and hour, the place and circumstances when they were born of God. They sing of the happy day when Jesus washed their sins away with a most definite memory of the inquiry-room where they sat, or of the altar at which they knelt, when "being justified by faith they had peace with God." Others, like the sainted Baxter, had no such experience. Gently as the sunlight breaks upon a sleeping world came the sweet influences of grace upon their youthful hearts. They know they love the Lord, but they do not remember when or where they entered into the kingdom. Let both classes beware. "The Spirit is not straitened" (Micah 2 : 7). To chalk off a definite line for the Spirit's manifold operations on the diversified character and conditions of men is a pernicious intruding of man within the realm of God. It has also the effect, when believed, of producing despondency in some minds and of creating a lack of charity in others.

The very diversity of operation shows the divinity. As we discover in nature an exuberant fulness and variety, and see in this the inexhaustible wealth of resources used by our Heavenly Father in Creation and Providence, so in the copiousness of grace, in the absence of restriction to one mode of operation, we discover the same divine richness—an opulent abundance of treasury equalled by an infinite variety of mode. Let, then, our Colonel Gardiners, "stopped in a moment in their mad career," respect the Richard Baxters who, in another way, came to the Saviour, and let not the Baxters reason from the way in which they were saved that that is the *only* way; and by criticism or assertion attempt to decry the Spirit's work in the sudden and startling conversion of men like Gardiner.

Two more evils appear in our modern Church life. One is in the hot-house culture of revived monasticism, where the highest perfection is supposed to be secured by Asceticism. The Church of Rome in teaching what she calls the Saviour's "Counsels of Perfection," claims that these—*chastity, poverty and obedience*—are only intended for a few favorites of Heaven. The application of the term "a religious" to monk or nun, interdicts the great mass of her followers from the hope of Christian perfection, lowers motherhood and fatherhood, and makes the religion of common things less attractive or possible.

This evil is nearer home than Rome. Let us watch most prayerfully and carefully the "Deaconness" and kindred movements in our common Protestantism, lest they leave the Scriptural foundation on which they rest and glide downward to monasticism.

> "We need not bid for cloistered cell
> Our neighbor and our work farewell,
> Or try to wind ourselves too high
> For sinful man beneath the sky.
>
> "The simple round, the common task,
> Will furnish all we ought to ask,
> Room to deny ourselves—a road
> To bring us daily nearer God."

Live amidst suffering men and spend your strength in helpful work. If men and women will thus learn to do the common things of life in a religious spirit—if they will open their eyes and recognize God's nearness to them and his help in the household duty, the office care or factory toil, they will cease grieving the Holy Spirit. My final word is upon grieving the Spirit in our failure of duty to our brother-man. We have often heard that "Man's inhumanity to man makes countless myriads mourn." It does more. It grieves the Holy Spirit. We who love the Lord are in the world *for his sake*, that we may witness for him; *for our own sake*, that we may grow in grace and be disciplined through suffering and work; but we are also here *for our brother's sake*.

No man, out of Christ, knows his own nature or his own worth. He does not know his danger. How then is this wide fringe of immortal men lying around the Churches to be reached and rescued? Not by pastors only, but *by every believer becoming a missionary.* When we realize that the Holy Spirit has burnt into our heart of hearts the conviction that we are in the world for the world's sake, and, taking up the cross, speak to those we know or meet on the claims of Christ,—on their relation to Eternity, on their own worth, estimated by the death of Jesus on the cross; then multitudes will be converted to God. "I will pour water upon him that is thirsty"—that is, the believer, conscious of his need, and knowing the source of supply; "And floods upon the dry ground"—that is, the mass of thoughtless and prayerless men reached when the Church is revived. Have you received a refreshing draught of the water of life? Then speak to others of Christ and the great salvation, and the energizing Spirit will accompany the word spoken in love. If men do not know their own worth we need not wonder that the world puts a low estimate upon the poor man. "What is he worth?" means money, not mental capacity or spiritual possibility. "What does he know," intellectual acquirement, not gifts of grace or soul-furnishing. Here the Church is being dominated by the world. Pray that our eyes may be opened to see the possible angel concealed in the sinner, as Angelo saw his great statue within the block of marble. Having faith in the Holy

Ghost, let us have faith in man. We can look upon the most depraved without despair, for they have a Saviour, and can be renewed by the Holy Spirit. As the father saved his money, about to be thrown in the fire by his thoughtless child, who knew not its value, let us rescue the perishing. "It is not the will of our Father in heaven that one of these little ones should perish." *His providence will give an opportunity and his Spirit a blessing.*

As but a moment ago the lighted gas burnt low, and this beautiful church, where once my rarely gifted friend, Thomas Guard preached the words of life, seemed gloomy and dull, and you could not read the Holy Book, but at the touch of an unseen janitor's hand, bright jets of flame flashed forth, and we now can see the glory of the fretted roof and the storied windows, or note the thoughtful faces of the devout worshippers. So may it be with ourselves and with our churches! We do not pray for more machinery, as this sacred place did not, an hour ago, need more gas fixtures. We have enough of church machinery. *We pray for more power.* Come, Holy Spirit, come! Clothe thy ministers with righteousness. Breathe into every heart thine own divine afflatus. Fill every service and agency with thy supreme and qualifying energy. Let an unction of the Holy One rest upon the people and the grieving, resisting and tempting of the Spirit of God shall cease.

X.

THE SPIRIT FOR WORSHIP AND WITNESSING.

BY D. M. STEARNS, SCRANTON, PA.

AS we consider the lack of real spiritual worship of God on the part of such multitudes of his professed people, and the "no worship at all" of the greater multitudes outside the church, the true worshipper is led to ask: "Will the time ever come when in all the world God shall be worshipped in spirit and in truth?" Assurance of success is to many a great inspiration, and if we can become fully persuaded that this time shall surely come, and that we shall see it, it may nerve us to seek more whole-heartedly for ourselves and others to be filled with the Spirit, that in this present time we may earnestly contend for true spiritual worship and testimony, standing resolutely apart from all dead forms and ceremonies, while we wait for, and seek to hasten, the dawn of a better dispensation than that in which we now live. If Abraham was enabled to wait more patiently by looking for the city which hath foundations; if Moses was enabled to turn away from all the attractions of Egypt's glory by getting his eyes and heart fixed on the recompense of the reward; if our Lord Jesus himself, "for the joy that was set before him, endured the cross;" we have the best of precedents to encourage ourselves by contemplating the grand consummation which is sure to come. Let us listen then for a few moments to the Spirit's own testimony as to what he will yet accomplish on our earth. "All the ends of the world shall remember, and turn unto the Lord; and all the kindreds of the nations shall worship before thee: for the kingdom is the Lord's, and he is the governor among the nations." "All the earth shall worship thee, and shall sing unto thee; they shall sing to thy name." "Yea, all kings shall fall down before him; all nations shall serve him." "All nations whom thou hast made shall come and worship before thee, O Lord; and shall glorify thy name." "And it shall come to pass, that from one new moon to another, and from one Sabbath to another, shall all flesh come to worship before me, saith the Lord." "And it shall come to pass, that every one that is left of all the nations which came against Jerusalem shall even go up from year to year to worship the King, the Lord of Hosts, and to keep the feast of Tabernacles." "Who shall not fear thee, O Lord, and glorify thy Name? for thou only art holy; for all nations shall come and worship before thee; for thy judgments are made manifest" (Ps. 22: 27, 28; 66: 4; 72: 11; 86: 9; Isa. 66: 23; Zec. 14: 16; Rev. 15: 4). If the question be asked "When shall these things be?" the Spirit, through Joel, plainly says that it will be after Jehovah has returned to dwell in the midst of Israel, that they may never again be ashamed, then will he pour out his Spirit upon all flesh; and that which had a germinant fulfilment at Pentecost shall have a complete and worldwide fulfilment when the kingdom shall be the Lord's. If it be asked "Who shall live when God doeth this?" the answer is "You who now hear these words if by faith in Christ Jesus and in the power of the Spirit you are a true worshipper of the Father."

It will help us in our worship now if we can form some idea of what worship will be in those days, and if we can get some light upon what true worship really is. Listen then to Seraphim and Cherubim, types of the most exalted portion of our redeemed humanity, the Church, the Body of Christ. "I saw the Lord sitting upon a Throne, high and lifted up, and his train filled the Temple. Above it stood the Seraphim; each one had six wings; with twain he covered his face, and with twain he covered his feet, and with twain he did fly. And one cried unto another and said, Holy, Holy, Holy is the Lord of Hosts; the whole earth is full of his Glory." "And the four living creatures had each of them six wings about him, and they were full of eyes within: and they rest not day and night, saying, Holy, Holy, Holy, Lord God Almighty, which was and is, and is to come. And when those living creatures give glory and honor and thanks to him that sat on the throne, who liveth for ever and ever, the four and twenty elders fall down before him that sat on the throne, and worship him that liveth for ever and ever, and cast their crowns before the throne, saying, Thou art worthy, O Lord, to receive glory and honor and power: for thou hast created all things, and for thy pleasure they are and were created." (Isa. 6: 1-3; Rev. 4: 8-11.) In these visions of Isaiah and John we see and hear true worship. The object of worship is a person, not a principle, or a creed, or a sect; not even an angel or an archangel; but the Lord himself, whom alone they exalt. The ground of worship is, "Thou wast slain, and hast redeemed us to God by thy blood, out of every kindred, and tongue, and people and nation; and hast made us unto our God Kings and Priests." The consummation is, "And we shall reign on the earth." The Power is seen in the seven lamps of fire burning before the throne, which are the seven Spirits of God, or the Spirit in his sevenfold fulness. (Rev. 5: 9, 10; 4: 5.) As to the worshippers, they do not boast of what they are, but cover their faces (indicating their characters) with their wings; they do not boast of what they have done, their Christian conduct or walk (indicated by the feet) but cover their feet also with their wings; and with one accord they vie with each other, as they cast their crowns before him, in extolling the Lord of Hosts, the Lord God Almighty, whose glory is the fulness of the whole earth.

Let us now descend from these glorious heights, this far-reaching mount of Transfiguration, and consider how we may worship and witness while we contend with the world, the flesh and the devil. Let us listen to the weary, lonely man, the God-man, God manifest in the flesh, the revealer of the Father, as he sits on Jacob's well and talks with the woman of Samaria. She being convinced of sin by the Spirit in him, seeks to evade the issue by bringing up the question of the place of worship; as if to-day one should say, well, it may be all true, but I do not believe as you do, I am a Catholic, or I am a Methodist, or a Baptist, or a Presbyterian, or an Episcopalian, you worship in your way and I'll worship in mine. Jesus replied that place or externals was nothing, but the heart everything; for the Father seeketh true worshippers, who shall worship in Spirit and in Truth. The woman had spoken of " Jacob our father" and of " our fathers," but Jesus speaks of "*The Father*," who alone is to be worshipped. While God is spoken of as " Father," a few times in the Old Testament, as in Ps. 89: 26; Isa. 63: 16; 64: 8, it remained for Jesus to reveal him as such, that as such we might worship him. It is the name by which we were first taught to address him, but how little we know of the fulness of the meaning of this beautiful name, and therefore how poor our worship. It is the name found in the first and last recorded utterances of Jesus, "Wist ye not that I must be about my Father's business?" "Father, into thy hands I commend my spirit" (Luke 2: 49; 23: 46); and it is the name first on his lips after his resurrection, when he says to Mary "Touch me not; for I am not yet ascended to my Father; but go to my brethren, and say unto them, I ascend unto my Father, and your Father; and to my God; and your God." (John 20: 17.) In his discourse and prayer on the night of his betrayal and arrest he uses the name about fifty times, saying among other things "He that hath seen me hath seen the Father—I am in the Father and the Father in me —at that day ye shall know that I am in my Father, and ye in me, and I in you." If we more fully realized our relationship to God as his children by faith in Christ Jesus, and his relationship to us as our Father who art in Heaven, then would our worship, both in public and private, be more real and more acceptable to him. This can be brought about only by the Holy Spirit. "For as many as are led by the Spirit of God, they are the sons of God . . . ye have received the Spirit of adoption, whereby we cry, Abba, Father." (Rom. 8: 14, 15.)

In over fifty of the 170 places where the Hebrew word for "worship" is found in the Old Testament, it is translated as "bow self down," and in this we have the whole hindrance to salvation, or life and service, or true worship. In the matter of the salvation of a sinner what is so great a hindrance as the mind of the flesh which is enmity against God; is not subject to the law of God, neither, indeed, can be: but takes pride in its own fancied righteousness, all of which is in God's sight only as filthy rags (Rom. 8: 7; Tit. 3: 5; Isa.

64 : 6). When the sinner has been enabled by the enlightening Spirit to see his filthiness and to renounce it, accepting in its place the spotless robe of the righteousness of God in Christ, what hinders the abundant life and service which every Christian ought to manifest, so much as this same self or flesh which remaining in the believer seeks to be pitied and pampered: and the believer instead of denying self, and mortifying the deeds of the body, putting off the old man, is, alas, too oft inclined to pity self (Matt. 16 : 22 marg.) instead of reckoning it dead (Rom. 6 : 11 ; 8 : 13 ; Matt. 16 : 24; 2 Cor. 4 : 11). Then as to worship, the difficulty is, confidence in the flesh, which is directly opposed to worshipping God in the Spirit and rejoicing in Christ Jesus (Phil. 3 : 3). They that are in the flesh cannot please God. No flesh shall glory in his presence. He that glorieth must glory in the Lord (Rom. 8 : 8 ; 1 Cor. 1 : 29-31).

We have been redeemed with the precious blood of Christ that we may yield ourselves fully unto him for his service, that by true worship and faithful testimony we may glorify God and win people to him as he has revealed himself in Jesus Christ. This we cannot do ; we are not sufficient for these things, but our sufficiency is of God who gives unto us the Holy Spirit to this end. He says, "Know ye not that ye are the temple of God, and that the Spirit of God dwelleth in you?" "What! know ye not that your body is the temple of the Holy Ghost which is in you, which ye have of God, and ye are not your own; for ye are bought with a price: therefore glorify God in your body and in your spirit, which are God's?" "Ye are the temple of the living God; as God hath said, I will dwell in them, and walk in them; and I will be their God, and they shall be my people" (1 Cor. 3:16; 6:19, 20; 2 Cor. 6:16). Then he adds, "Wherefore come out from among them, and be ye separate, saith the Lord, and touch not the unclean; and I will receive you, and will be a Father unto you, and ye shall be my sons and daughters, saith the Lord Almighty." This is the only place in the New Testament outside the book of Revelation where we find the name "Almighty;" and its use here is most interesting and instructive, and right in the line of our subject. The name "Almighty" signifies literally "the breasted one" (Shaddai); and reveals God to us as the all-sufficient pourer forth of all temporal and spiritual blessings. It is first found in Gen. 17:1, after a blank in Abram's history of thirteen years because of his reliance on the flesh instead of on the all-sufficient Jehovah. Then Jehovah comes to him saying, "I am the Almighty God, walk before me, and be thou perfect (or upright, or sincere)." Then is his name changed from Abram (exalted father) to Abraham (father of a multitude). The middle letter of Elohim, and the principal letter of Jehovah, God's great name, is inserted in Abram's name, as if to indicate that God in him would now cause him to be fruitful. Of the less than sixty times that the name "Almighty" is found in the whole Bible, it is found more than half the number (31 times) in the book of Job; where we have the history of a servant of God, thoroughly emptied of himself; and thus ceasing to think anything of himself, and leaning on the sufficiency of the Almighty pourer forth, everything is literally doubled to him. Oh, how fruitful our worship and testimony would be, and how glorifying to God, if we would only separate ourselves from all filthiness of the flesh and spirit, perfecting holiness in the fear of God (2 Cor. 7:1); and thus allowing our Almighty Father to prove himself our sufficiency, how gloriously he would show to the world that such Christians are indeed his sons and daughters; and how he would delight to show forth his power in them and on their behalf.

We must remember that there can be no acceptable worship or testimony apart from the sacrifice of the Lord Jesus, or the sacrifices which, before he came, pointed forward to his; for "without shedding of blood is no remission" (Heb. 9:22), and the unsaved cannot worship God. In the offerings of Cain and Abel there was a foreshadowing of all future worshippers and their methods. Those who do not see their guilt and their need of a substitute come as Cain came, bringing the best they have, well satisfied with themselves; but there is no worship, for there is no atonement, and their offerings, however beautiful, are not accepted by God. Those who like Abel see their guilt, and come in humble reliance upon the Lamb slain for them, rejoicing in the blood that was shed for their sins, as they sing,

> "Nothing in my hands I bring,
> Simply to thy cross I cling."

These are acceptable worshippers.

In our public worship our services consist of Praise, Prayer, Preaching and an Offering, and the Spirit has not left us without guidance in reference to each part. "I will pray with the Spirit, and I will pray with the understanding also; I will sing with the Spirit and I will sing with the understanding also. . . . I had rather speak five words with my understanding, that I might teach others also, than ten thousand words in an unknown tongue." "They read in the book, in the law of God distinctly, and gave the sense, and caused them to understand the reading" (1 Cor. 14: 15, 19; Neh. 8: 8). Here are the Spirit's own directions for the worship of God, and if we are to worship in Spirit it must be in submission to the Spirit's guidance. All must be done that all may be benefited and all take part in the worship. We will suppose that those who lead the praise of the congregation are Christian men and women, for otherwise they have no right to any such place, inasmuch as the unsaved cannot worship: "They that are in the flesh cannot please God" (Rom. 8: 8): now if they sing that which the congregation cannot take part in, where is the worship on the part of the congregation? Then when the minister prays, if the congregation do not in their hearts endorse every petition, where is the prayer on their part? And as to the preaching, if it is not simple enough for the most unlearned to receive, where is the benefit? When we sing let us sing only what we mean with our whole hearts, for is it not as sinful to sing a lie as to tell a lie? When we pray let us ask for what we really want for God's glory, and expect to receive it. And when we speak let us hear the word at God's mouth and give them warning from him; or when we hear let us desire to hear only what God has to say to us and not the opinions of men. As to the offering, which is as much a part of the worship as the prayer or praise or preaching, here is the Spirit's guidance. "Every man according as he purposeth in his heart, so let him give; not grudgingly or of necessity: for God loveth a cheerful giver.' "Of every man that giveth it willingly with his heart shall ye take my offering" (2 Cor. 9: 7; Ex. 25: 2). Let me think of myself as an individual worshipper, whether in pulpit or pew, what is my aim, what my motive? The only proper aim is to glorify God, to exalt him, to make him known; the motive, the love of Christ constraining; the motto, "Unto him who loved me and washed me from my sins in his own blood" (Rev. 1: 5); the power, his Spirit who dwelleth in me. I go to the house of God, persistently shutting out the world and worldly things, that I may praise him, talk with him, hear him talk to me, and thus commune with him. Is it time to sing? then I am to sing with my whole heart unto the Lord. Is it time to pray? then

I am to make my soul's desire known to him with thanksgiving. Is it time to speak or hear? then I am to speak his word, or watch to see what he (not the speaker) will say unto me or in me. Is it time for the offering? then I am to give unto him with a willing and grateful heart, such an offering as I would not be ashamed to place in his own hand; he knowing what he has given to me, how much I am reserving for myself, and how much I ought cheerfully to give unto him. In all this there is not the slightest room for the flesh, or for the praise of man; it is from beginning to end, "Unto him," because of his love to me, and in the power of his Spirit. This, and nothing less than this, is, as far as I can learn from the Scriptures, worshipping the Father in Spirit and in Truth.

In reference to witnessing, we must look unto him who is "the Amen, the faithful and true witness" (Rev. 3:14), whose life was the light of men. He who was the Light of the world says to us who believe in him, "Ye are the light of the world." We are to walk as he walked, to reproduce his life in these mortal bodies. As there can be no life or light without something being consumed, so we must be willing to present our bodies a living sacrifice that the Spirit may consume us with earnest desire for the glory of God. Not our own will or pleasure or glory, but in all things the will, the pleasure, the glory of God. With such lives we shall be qualified to speak of him, and be bearers of the glad tidings of the kingdom to others who have not yet heard the gospel. A witness must be able to say, "I know," "I am fully persuaded," "I speak that which I know and testify that which I have seen" (2 Tim. 1: 12; Rom. 4: 21; John 3: 11; 1 John 1: 1-3), and he must be ready also to lay down his life for the truth, to be a "*martyr*," for such is the word for "witness" (Rev. 2: 13). Jesus testified of the necessity of being born from above; the necessity of being willing to forsake all for him; the necessity of being willing to suffer with him, denying self and bearing the cross daily; the necessity of living here for the sake of the good we may do in his Name, separating ourselves from the world. He taught that at death the believer goes out into conscious happiness, the unbeliever into conscious torment, and that there is no possibility of exchanging places after death, that the ungodly dying in their sins cannot reach the place of the blest. He taught that we are not rewarded for our works at death, but at the resurrection of the just. He taught that he will come again in power and great glory, and that then will be the restoration and redemption of Israel. He taught us to watch constantly for his return, expecting him any hour. If we are to be his witnesses, filled with his Spirit, we must continue to reiterate all that he taught, not omitting a single truth. He did not teach that his coming meant death, or that the kingdom is the church, and that the kingdom has come: but he did teach that his coming meant "not to die," and that the kingdom is postponed till his return (John 21: 22, 23; Luke 19: 11-15).

From all this we can see that to worship God in Spirit and Truth, and to be a faithful witness, requires more power than mortal man was ever possessed of, and were it not that the power for this life and testimony is placed by God within reach of all we might well despair of ever attaining to it. "Tarry until ye be endued with power from on high:" "Ye shall receive power, after that the Holy Ghost is come upon you, and ye shall be witnesses unto me" (Luke 24:49; Acts 1:8), were some of his last words to those who had been with him for three years; and if they needed this power who had seen him face to face and had already wrought miracles in his name, how much more do we? To show how ready he is to bestow this gift he has said, "If ye then being evil, know how to give good gifts to your children, how much more shall your Heavenly Father give the Holy Spirit to them that ask him?" (Luke 11:13).

If any should still ask, "How may I obtain it?" I should say, Importunately seek it with your whole heart for his glory, and not for any selfish end; be willing to be emptied and cleansed that he may fill you, and if you fear you are not willing, ask him to make you willing: remember that it is written, "We who live are always delivered unto death for Jesus' sake, that the life also of Jesus might be made manifest in our mortal flesh" (2 Cor. 4:11), and therefore take delight in every opportunity to mortify the flesh. Cling in helplessness as Jacob with his thigh out of joint clung to the mighty One. Watch as intently as Elisha watched Elijah before they were separated. When any one thus seeks with the whole heart to be filled with the Holy Spirit for the Glory of God they shall surely be filled; learn to worship God in Spirit and Truth, and become faithful witnesses.

Let no one say, It is not for me, or It will cost too much; you are not your own, and you are commanded to be filled with the Spirit (Eph. 5: 18); if you refuse, you are disobedient and the loss you will never know till it is too late to regain it. Let each one say, "I am thine, O Lord." "I yield fully unto thee." "Make me a vessel meet for thy service." Take the blessing by faith and go forth in his Name.

XI.

THE SPIRIT IN AGREEMENT WITH THE WORD.

W. J. ERDMAN.

THE so-called Christian world is full of religious "views," vagaries of doctrine, revelations and interpretations, all professedly received from the Spirit of God; is there any test whereby to decide the reality of the Spirit's presence and action?

In answer, the subject is at present limited to the relation of the Spirit to the Word, as to doctrine, morals, and leading in life and service.

It is evident, from a comparison of the two exhortations, each allied to a similar context, "Be filled with the Spirit," Eph. 5: 18, and, "Let the word of Christ dwell in you richly," Col. 3: 16, that neither the Spirit alone, nor the Word alone is enough. The Spirit, however, with but little truth in the knowledge of the believer is effective in life and in service, while much truth—yea, all truth, without the Spirit, remains but a dead letter. True is the warning and greatly to be heeded concerning the danger of "traffic in unfelt truth."

The Spirit enlightens to understand the Word; the Word tests the professed action of the Spirit. The gift of "discerning of spirits" must now be substituted by the knowledge of the Word; an Aquila and Priscilla may take aside and expound unto an eloquent Apollos the way of God more perfectly.

I. AS TO DOCTRINE.

a. How to test all teaching: Christ Jesus the touchstone. 1 Cor. 12: 3, negatively, "No man speaking by the Spirit of God calleth Jesus accursed" (anathema), a deceiver, an impostor, one who justly was put to death for blasphemous claims of divinity and Messiahship; positively, "And no man can say that Jesus is the Lord, but by the Holy Ghost." This Scripture decides concerning the truth of much religious teaching and experience of the present day. It is stated again in 1 John 4: 1-3, which gives the key to 1 John 2: 20, 27. The readers of this epistle had the Holy Spirit, indeed, not to dispense with the teaching of John, or of any inspired or enlightened man, but in order to understand what John wrote, even that the historic Jesus was none other than the Life Eternal. In him as such they were to abide, and as such to know they had received the unction from the Holy One; the Spirit, the all illumining oil from Christ. Not so to abide in Christ, but to go forward, progress (not transgress 2 John 9), was the characteristic of deceivers—anti-christs; and what a test of teaching is this word "progresses" in this present time of ' progressive," "broad," "liberal" theology.

b. How to learn the true teaching: Jesus illustrates the Spirit's method and law of learning.

THE SPIRIT IN AGREEMENT WITH THE WORD. 119

Compare concerning the sufferings, death, burial and resurrection of Christ the word "teach" in Mark 8:31 and "shew" in Matt. 16:21. Jesus brought together predictions and types of the Old Testament, pointing them out, and so taught the disciples. Paul's "proving" in Acts 9:22 signifies a demonstrating, a proving by joining together the old Scriptures concerning the Messiah, and so arriving at the infallible conclusion. The much-praised Baconian, inductive method, is no new thing; the Bible is always ahead. Compare also " the opening and alledging" of Acts 17:3.

To this method of study, to this concentering of all scattered rays into a focus, the Spirit of God has promised his presence and guidance: "In thy light we shall see light."

And the word "guide"—show the way, or lead in the way—found but twice in the New Testament, gives an additional hint. Jesus said of the Spirit, "He will guide you into or in all the truth"—*i. e.*, concerning himself, the Truth, John 16:21, and the illustration is given in Philip, when the Eunuch of Ethiopia replied, "How can I, except some man should guide me?" Acts 8:26–40.

No word has been of such a help in the study of the Bible as the word "again," found in Matt. 4:7, where Jesus answers the Devil's quotation of Scripture with, "It is written again." That word holds the balances of divine truth; it is the corrective of all theory; it is the clinch of all statement. Suppose a certain doctrine to be provable by seven texts. One man knowing only four may indeed have hold of the doctrine, but it will be in disproportioned shape; even six will set forth a defective statement; all seven are needed to present the truth in full and rounded form.

Another danger besetting the study and application of the Word is the insertion into the text or collection of passages of some unwarranted inference or conclusion in the interest of some supposed lack of harmony or consistence of teaching. It is better to wait until the harmony is created by the Spirit in his own marvellous way.

How many have made shipwreck of the faith by mistaking certain fanciful, visionary "signs" and hallucinations as the work and suggestion of the Holy Spirit of Truth.

II. AS TO MORALS.

The Spirit never leads one to transgress fundamental law. He never urges one or suggests to one to commit murder, theft, adultery, to offer up human sacrifices, to steal or borrow money—never intending to repay until such time as the Spirit again may suggest, to be allied to "affinities" and "spiritual wives;" no matter what seeming signs and wonders, or visions and voices may appear to attest all.

The Spirit of God is *holy*, and his fruit holy, Galat. 5: 18.

III. AS TO LEADING IN DAILY LIFE AND SERVICE.

There is no "Urim and Thummim" now; no voices and visions external to instruct; only suggestions and convictions internal. But no rule can one lay down for others. Each has his own secret with the Lord, and it is best not always, if ever, to say to others, The Lord led me; the Lord sent me. The Lord has too often thereby been charged with folly. The Word, and often also common sense, must confirm and verify the secret suggestion. There do come times and occasions when it is most meet to declare how the Lord led one, but silence also has its times.

1. No one should try to run the experiences of others into the mould of his own. The very presence of the Spirit is not manifested in all and through all alike. To some, as Mr. Finney himself said, the Spirit's coming or manifestation is like the slowly opening dawn, to others like a burst of sunlight through rifted clouds at noonday; to some like the gentle dew, to others like a storm and tempest of rain. The pouring of the love of God into our hearts as Father is often, if not always, the first or positive manifestation of the Spirit; it is precedent to or at least concomitant with "the enduement of power."

2. The Spirit controls events, and therefore desires us to "redeem the time," Eph. 5: 16, *i. e.*, study opportunities for ministry, monopolize occasions, "make a corner" of times and providences.

All this implies not a passive, inert condition of soul, but one pliant, adjustable, quick-turning like Cherubim.

3. The Spirit, for one earnest, willing and ready to

serve, *prepares* for service in our ordinary work and daily routine of duty. One does not need to be on the rack of inquiry where and what to do.

The annals of Christian ministry abound in illustrations of this truth.

4. The Spirit will bring to remembrance ordinary and extraordinary things, if so the need be. But note, it says, "Bring to *remembrance.*" The preacher who declares all that is necessary is to "open the mouth and the Lord will fill it," sooner or later will learn to his sorrow that the Lord fills the mouth out of the head, and not out of the fist.

"Perspiration is not inspiration." "Exposition is sometimes imposition." Said a theological teacher to a student who talked of dropping certain studies and taking a "short-cut" to the ministry, "Young man, how much ignorance do you suppose it takes to make a minister?"

4. Last of all, in order to be sure of the correctness of convictions concerning duties and affairs domestic or public, or in regard to the assurance of answers to prayer, it is not only necessary to try them by the Word, by providences, by common sense, by the experience of other Christians, but especially is necessary an equipoise of mind, a self-emptiedness of heart an equipoise which is the result of a willingness to have the will of God done either way.

The soul must settle down to a waveless calm, and so clearly reflect the mind of God. Such equipoise and mirroring of soul are certainly implied, as well as the inflowing power of fruitful service, in the words, "If ye abide in me and my words abide in you, ye shall ask what ye will and it shall be done unto you." John 15: 7.

More than all, how full of comfort the Word, that when we know not what we should pray for as we ought, the Spirit takes up the case and makes intercession according to the will of God. Rom. 8: 26–28.

XII.

THE HOLY SPIRIT AND THE CHRISTIAN.

F. M. ELLIS, D.D.

THE fact that "the Baptism of the Holy Spirit"— "the promise of the Father" and "Special gift of the Son"—*follows the "new birth"*—which Jesus, in his conversation with Nicodemus, explained as being "born of the Spirit," and furthermore, that such terms as "Baptized with the Holy Spirit," "The Holy Spirit fell on them," "The Holy Spirit came," "Receive ye the Holy Spirit," "The power of the Holy Spirit," The fellowship of the Holy Spirit, etc., are only applied to believers in Christ, unite to invest with more than ordinary interest the topic assigned me—

"THE HOLY SPIRIT AND THE CHRISTIAN."

While the general statement of this topic might warrant a wide range of treatment, it will be our aim, as far as possible, to confine ourselves to a strictly Scriptural treatment of it. In this discussion we shall confine ourselves to the New Testament; and in our quotations shall use the *"new version"*—using the terms *"Holy Spirit"* rather than the terms *"Holy Ghost"*— as we believe this better expresses the original.

THE HOLY SPIRIT AND THE CHRISTIAN.

The tide of modern thought, that has so long swept about the person and work of Christ, seems, on its return, to be becoming more concerned with the person and work of the Holy Spirit. From the Christ, "the organ of external revelation," attention is being turned to the Holy Spirit—"the organ of internal revelation." From the Advocate *for* us, who *is with the Father*, Christians are earnestly asking to know more of the advocate *with us*, who is *here among us*.

Whatever opinions may have place in our minds as to the meaning and application of the words of the Baptist: "He that cometh after me is mightier than I. . . . He shall baptize you with the Holy Spirit and with fire"—we are all agreed that there is, at least, an implied promise in these words of a richer blessing and a far larger equipment for service than that enjoyed by average Christians to-day.

If the statement of Bishop Hopkins be accepted as the true interpretation of the Baptist's meaning—that "those who are baptized with the Holy Spirit are, as it were, plunged into the heavenly flame, whose searching energy devours all their dross, tin and base alloy," then certainly we may conclude that too many, who have a place in our Churches, like the disciples at Ephesus, "have not so much as heard whether there be any Holy Spirit" (Acts 19: 2). And especially are we thus impressed when we call to mind our Lord's promise, "ye shall receive power when the Holy Spirit is come upon you" (Acts 1: 8). If an endowment of power be inseparable from the baptism of the Holy Spirit, then surely the confessed and lamentable absence of such power among us ought to occasion the most serious concern upon the part of all who have "named the name of the Lord."

In no age, possibly, have Christian Churches been so well equipped for effective service for Christ as they are now. Like marvelous structures of ingenious machinery, our churches stand forth—endowed with wealth, enriched with education, culture and social influence—possessing splendid church edifices, elaborate music and rituals, sound in creeds, confessions and covenants. And yet, alas! these numerous and admirable channels carry but driveling streams of that divine energy that made the early churches such centres of evangelizing power—when they were composed of disciples whose faith stood not in "the words which man's wisdom teacheth, but which the Holy Spirit teacheth." The crying need of the age is not more of such churches, or more or better appliances, but a universal baptism of the Holy Spirit. Were this given, the church could, with her present resources, give the gospel to the world within the next decade.

It goes without saying, therefore, that the relation of the Holy Spirit to the Christian is a most vital and important one. For it is to such as are taught by the Spirit to discern things spiritual that the Christ is revealed, and to such only. If, *e.g.*, it had been revealed to Simeon that "he should not see death until he had seen the Lord's Christ" (Luke 2: 26), it was because before that "the Holy Spirit was upon him."

The promise of Jesus that God would bestow the gift of the Holy Spirit could not be more freely made —indeed, he places the Father under obligations of love, greater than that of parental affection, to do so.

"If ye then, being evil, know how to give good gifts to your children, *how much more* shall your heavenly Father give the Holy Spirit to them that ask him" (Luke 11: 13; Jno. 7: 37–39). If, then, we are without this blessed endowment, it is certainly not because the Father is unwilling to grant it. It must be because we do not ask for it. Or if we ask, because we ask amiss.

While the gifts of the Holy Spirit may fall upon the church at large, as the sunshine falls upon the plain, after all these gifts emphasize the personal duty and responsibility of believers as that sunlight burnishes and beautifies each separate object on the wide plain.

The gifts of the Holy Spirit, however, are not the monopoly of ordained teachers, nor the special trust of the few gifted ones, but the priceless gift of God *to believers* as such.

On the evening of the day on which our Lord rose from the dead, when he had met his disciples, and had shown them his hands and his side, "the disciples were glad when they saw the Lord; Jesus, therefore, said unto them again, Peace be unto you; as the Father hath sent me, even so send I you, and when he had said this, he breathed on them, and said unto them, Receive ye the Holy Spirit." (Jno. 20 : 20, 23.) Thus Jesus recognized, in his gift, no official claim or ecclesiastical superiority. "He breathed on them"—*the disciples.*

So also on the day of Pentecost, when "they were all together in one place," the descending Spirit "sat upon each of them, and they were *all filled* with the Holy Spirit, and began to speak with tongues as the Spirit gave them utterance." (Acts 2: 1–4.)

Nor was this fulfillment of "the promise of the Father" confined to those from "*the upper room;*" for even to those who, "pricked in the heart," cried out "what shall we do?" Peter replied, "Repent ye, and be baptized, *every one* of you, in the name of Jesus Christ, unto the remission of your sins, and ye shall receive the gift of the Holy Spirit." (Acts 2 : 37–38.)

And later on, when Peter and John, being dismissed from the Sanhedrim, had related to "the company of the disciples" what the chief priests and elders had said unto them, the record is—"when they had prayed the place was shaken wherein they had gathered together, and *they were all filled* with the Holy Spirit, and they spake the word of God with boldness." (Acts 4: 31.) On another occasion, when before the council, Peter, on behalf of the disciples, bore this testimony—"We are witnesses of these things, and so is the Holy Spirit, whom God hath given to *all them that obey him.*" (Acts 5 : 32.) After this, when persecution had scattered abroad the church at Jerusalem ("*ex-*

cept *the Apostles*"), and the disciples went about preaching the word, Philip went down to the City of Samaria, and so preached Christ there that "the multitudes gave heed to his testimony," and "the city was filled with joy." The news of this wonderful work soon reached the Apostles at Jerusalem, and they sent Peter and John down to Samaria, "who, when they were come down, prayed for them, that they might receive the Holy Spirit. . . . then laid they their hands on them, and they (the Samaritans) received the Holy Spirit" (Acts 8: 18).

By the laying on of Ananias' hands Saul received the Holy Spirit.

Peter testifies respecting Cornelius and his household, "As I began to speak the Holy Spirit fell *on them, even as on us at the* beginning" (Acts 11: 15). This statement he reiterates before the Apostles and brethren at Jerusalem (Acts 15: 8, 9). So also Paul bestowed the gift of the Holy Spirit upon the "*twelve brethren*," whom he found at Ephesus. (Acts 19: 6.)

Thus upon those who "believed the testimony of God to his Son" was this gift of the Holy Spirit given—and that, too, not for the comfort and happiness of those who thus received it, but for *witness—testimony—service.*

God makes no gifts to us, much less does he give us the Holy Spirit to be a mere selfish luxury. The Spirit's gift is one of life and power, and these are for use, and not for personal gratification merely. With the privileges of this gift comes the most solemn and responsible ordination God has ever given to man.

No qualification is so important or more practical to the Christian as this gift of the Holy Spirit.

Looking forward to those coming days of trial, when brother would deliver brother to death, when parents should betray children and children would persecute parents, Jesus said: "When they lead you to judgment and deliver you up, be not anxious beforehand what ye shall speak, but whatsoever shall be given you *in that hour, that speak* ye, for it is not ye that speak, but the Holy Spirit." (Mark 12: 11; Luke 12: 11-12.) For the full assurance and illustration of this promise of the Master we have but to turn to that marvelous "gospel of the Holy Spirit," the book of the "Acts of the Apostles."

These relations of the Holy Spirit to the early Christians are sufficient to illustrate what his relations are to Christians of all ages.

In applying what has been said to the subject in hand let us consider—

I. What the Holy Spirit *is to the Christian.*

1. Without the Holy Spirit a Christian would be *an impossibility.*

The Apostle lays down as unquestionable this statement: "Wherefore I give you to understand that *no man* speaking in the spirit of God saith Jesus is anathema, and *no man can say that Jesus is Lord* but by the Holy Spirit" (1 Cor. 12: 13).

This test of the absolute need of the Holy Spirit, even in the full confession of Jesus Christ, applied to the Corinthian Christians no more fully than it does to Christians *now*. This statement of Paul is thus reaffirmed by John: "Hereby know ye the Spirit of God; every spirit that confesseth that Jesus Christ has come in the flesh is of God; and every spirit that confesseth not that Jesus Christ is come in the flesh is not of God" (1 John 4: 2). The Holy Spirit came into the world, not only "to glorify Christ," but to manifest himself in those who "honor the Son even as they honor the Father." I need not say this question is not one of *physical* ability, but one of honest, loving loyalty to Jesus Christ as Master and Lord. It is not the creed or ordinance that makes the Christian. We are Christians just so far as we love, serve and honor the Lord Jesus Christ, and we can do this only as we are taught and aided by the Holy Spirit.

"Every good gift and every perfect gift," says James, "is from above." Further on he says, "Of his own will begat he us by the word of truth" (2: 18). Referring to the influence of the word in regeneration, Paul says, "Knowing, brethren, beloved of God, your election, how that our gospel came not unto you in word only, but also in power, *and in the Holy Spirit,* and in much assurance; even as ye know what manner of men we showed ourselves toward you, for your sake, and ye became imitators of us and the Lord; having received the Word in much affliction, with joy of the Holy Spirit" (1 Thess.

1 : 5–6). If further proof be needed of this essential relation of the Holy Spirit to the Christian, as the Quickener of those "dead in trespasses and sins," and hence of the fact that, apart from the Holy Spirit, the Christian life would be impossible, we have it in the following exhaustive summary. After showing what man is as a subject of the "powers of darkness," before he is made "meet to be partaker of the inheritance of the saints in light," the Apostle says, "But when the kindness of God our Saviour, and his love toward man appeared, not by works done in righteousness, which we did ourselves, but according to his mercy he saved us, through the washing of regeneration and renewing of the Holy Spirit, which he poured out upon us richly through Jesus Christ our Saviour, that being justified by his grace we might be made heirs according to the hope of eternal life" (Titus 3: 4–7).

Jesus said to Nicodemus, "Except a man be born anew he cannot see the kingdom of God." This our Lord explains thus: "That which is born of the flesh *is flesh*, and that which is born of the Spirit *is* Spirit" (John 3: 36). The necessity of being born of the Spirit to enter upon a spiritual life is as necessary as *natural birth* is for entrance into the natural life.

2. As Christians we have our access to God by the Holy Spirit.

While it is said that we who were once *afar off* were brought nigh "in the blood of Christ," it is also said, "Through him (*i. e.,* Christ) "we have our access in *one Spirit* unto the Father" (Eph. 2: 18).

The death of Christ gave to all, Jew and Gentile alike, audience with a reconciled Father, through the merits of Christ. Jesus Christ is the only name whereby we can be saved, because no man can come unto the Father except through him. To the Christ who presents us to God, we must be presented by the Holy Spirit.

"Through Christ we bring our message to the Father by the Spirit's aid." "For the Spirit helpeth our infirmity, for we know not *how to pray as we ought*, but the Spirit himself maketh intercession for us with groanings that cannot be uttered, and he that searcheth the hearts knoweth what is the mind of the Spirit, because he maketh intercession for us according to the will of God" (Rom. 8: 26).

If the petitions we bring to the Father, through the Son, are acceptable, therefore, they must voice the intercession of the Holy Spirit. "The searcher of hearts" must find in our prayers the mind of the Spirit, for he only can "make intercession according to the will of God." On the other hand, prayer in the Holy Spirit will not be denied by the Father. Jude exhorts us, in these words, "But ye, beloved, building up yourselves on your most holy faith, praying in the Holy Spirit, keep yourselves in the love of God, looking for the mercy of our Lord Jesus Christ unto eternal life" (20, 21).

We may not translate "infirmity" into such terms as "indifference," "known sin," and the like, and expect the "help" of the Holy Spirit in our intercession and prayers. He dwells not where he is not wanted. If he teaches us "*how to pray,*" if he reveals unto us the things of the Christ, and thus makes known to us the will of God, we must not grieve him by an habitual neglect of the word of God, for the Holy Spirit honors the Christ by honoring his word—through that divine word the divine Spirit reaches the Christian. In such things as hinder those who earnestly and honestly seek God's will in his word, the Holy Spirit will give his aid. But he nowhere promises his help to those who refuse compliance with the terms on which he offers his help.

3. Consider the Spirit's relation to the Christian *as a witness.* He does not bear witness to the Christian *of his conversion.* The word bears that witness. But the Spirit does bear witness to the believer's adoption or Sonship. The gospel is not a "message of bondage to fear," but a revelation of the liberty and heirship of believers as the sons and daughters of God. To this testimony of the word the Holy Spirit adds his blessed witness.

"For ye have received," says Paul, "the spirit of adoption, whereby ye cry, Abba Father, the Spirit beareth witness with *our* spirit that we are the children of God, and if children, then heirs, heirs of God, and joint heirs with Jesus Christ" (Rom. 8: 15–17).

Again, the Holy Spirit also witnesses to the presence of the Christ in the believer. "Hereby we know that he abideth in us by the Spirit which he gave us"

(1 Jno. 3 : 24). And again, "Hereby know we that we abide in him, and he in us, because he hath given us of his Spirit" (1 Jno. 4 : 13).

So fully was the Apostle Paul given up to the guidance of the Holy Spirit that he submitted his conscience to his leading. He never said that he was to be followed in anything, because he was conscientious in what he said or did. What does he say? listen, " I say the truth in Christ; I lie not, my conscience bearing witness with me *in the Holy Spirit* " (Rom. 9 : 1). Such a conscience, thus enlightened and in harmony with the truth in Christ, and with the witness of the Holy Spirit, any Christian may follow. But before we pronounce upon the accuracy of the decisions of our conscience, let us be sure that our conscience is in accord with the " truth in Christ," and the Holy Spirit's *infallible witness*.

Only as the Christian has the witness of the Spirit to his adoption as a son of God will the kingdom of God be anything more than " eating and drinking, ordinances and ceremonies, rights and works," and become what it really is, " Righteousness, and peace, and joy in the Holy Spirit" (Rom. 14 : 17).

These are the fruit of the Spirit in Christian living that give forth the fragrance of grace here, and will ripen eventually in the kingdom of Christ's glory.

4. Let us dwell a moment on the relation of the Holy Spirit to the believer *as " the Comforter,"* thus further showing *what he is to the Christian*. The send-

ing of the Comforter was to be more than a compensation for the departure of Jesus. True, they were not to be left "*desolate*." "If I go not away the Comforter will not come unto you, but if I go away I will send him unto you" (Jno. 16:7). Christ was still to be nearer them even than he could be by his personal presence; for his personal presence was limited to locality. Whereas when the Comforter came he would not be restricted by any such limitation. "Wherever two or three were met in his name," there would he be "in the midst of them." He was to "abide with them forever" as "the Spirit of Truth." "Moreover," said Jesus, "the Comforter, even the Holy Spirit, whom the Father will send in my name, he shall teach you all things, and bring to your remembrance all things that I have said unto you" (Jno. 14:16-26). As the divine presence was the glory of the Temple of old, so of these regenerated disciples, who were to be the Temples of the Holy Spirit, their glory would be his indwelling. If the manifestation of the divine glory of the Old Temple was awful and glorious in its outward revelations, the manifestation of the divine Paraclete, in the disciples of Christ, was to be much more glorious in his inner teachings and blessed consolations. Hence Jesus said, "It is expedient for you that I go away." We therefore undervalue these words of our Lord when we suppose that the time of his personal presence among his disciples was the most favored period of the Church's history. This was not as our Lord thought;

on the contrary, he himself taught us to look for the Comforter's administration as an advance upon his ministry; and as being a greater blessing to his people than that of his personal companionship with them. "Greater things than these shall ye do because I go unto the Father." The Comforter was more than an emanation from the Father, or an indefinable influence; he is more than a principle of spiritual life in believers; he is a living person, and hence we may not degrade him into a mere abstraction or influence, even though these misconceptions of his divine personality be dignified by such terms as "*the enthusiasm of humanity.*" He is the divine Spirit of Truth leading the believer into all truth—the Holy Spirit producing in those whom he leads the fruit of holiness: in a word, the fruit of the Spirit which "is in all goodness and righteousness and truth" (Eph. 5:9). The word never confounds "the fruit of the Spirit" with "the works of the flesh"—"*fruit*" belongs to the Spirit: "works" to the flesh. We need to have a care, therefore, in our thought of the personality of the Holy Spirit lest we lose sight of his person in vague ideas of him that maintain a place in our minds by means of terms the most general and indefinite. So also we need to have definite ideas of his specific work as well as of his person. It is the Holy Spirit who imparts spiritual life, quickens and sustains it—who gives strength, implants hope, grants liberty; testifies to and glorifies the Christ; leads, guides, teaches, comforts, sanctifies, supports and sustains the believer. As Christ is the foundation of faith, and the source of all merit, so the Holy Spirit is the fountain of all spiritual life. Until he imparts to the soul spiritual life, we are incapable of the exercise of that faith that lays hold on the person and work of Christ for justification and eternal life.

After quoting Isaiah as saying, "Things which the eye saw not, and ear heard not, and which entered not into the heart of man, whatsoever things God prepared for those who loved him," Paul adds these words, "But unto us God revealed them through the Spirit; for the Spirit searcheth all things, yea, the deep things of God" (1 Cor. 2: 9, 10). This is certainly an advance upon the revelation of Christ's ministry—what Jesus taught the Holy Spirit makes to be understood. Indeed, the advent of the Holy Spirit is the final and most glorious manifestation of God that will be granted the world, or the Church, until his dispensation will be superseded by the Second Advent of our Lord as the "*King of Saints.*"

When the care of the Churches so weighed upon the great apostle of the Gentiles as to press him to his knees upon the cold stone floor of his Roman prison— when his heart was bleeding at the thought of the trials of their faith, with hands that moved slowly because of the chains that bound them, he traced in letters of cheer and instruction, such words as these, punctuated by his tears, "For this cause I bow my knees unto the Father . . . that he would grant you, according to the riches of his glory, that ye may be strengthened with power through his Spirit in the inward man" (Eph. 3 : 14–16). Such was the help which the apostle sought from the Comforter for his brethren. Such is the comfort we all need, and this help the Comforter has for us also.

Thus the Christian who is chosen "according to the foreknowledge of God the Father, in sanctification of the Spirit, unto obedience and sprinkling of the blood of Jesus Christ" (1 Peter 1 : 2), who enters the kingdom of God by being "born of the Spirit," and who is "washed, sanctified and justified in the name of the Lord Jesus Christ, and in the Spirit of our God" (1 Cor. 6: 11), must, "through the Spirit, by faith, wait for the hope of the righteous" (Gal. 5 : 5).

Having considered what the Holy Spirit *is to the Christian*, let us

II. Consider what the Holy Spirit *does for the Christian*.

Being, by the grace of God, made partakers of the Holy Spirit, we become the special objects of the Holy Spirit's love, care and culture. And since our love for God, and God's love for us, are in a sense reciprocal—for "we love him because he first loved us," and because "God is love," and because "he that abideth in love abideth in God, and God in him" (1 Jno. 4: 16)—the Holy Spirit, who first awakens, also develops this love for God in us; "because," says Paul, "the love of God hath been shed abroad in our hearts through the Holy Spirit which was given unto us" (Rom 5 : 5). As an illustration of this, you may remember how Epaphras refreshed Paul when he declared unto him "*the love in the Spirit*" of the brethren at Colosse.

The influence of the Holy Spirit in thus awakening in us the highest possible form of love, is absolutely indispensable. Grant that the natural affections are the soil out of which this love of the Christian for God is produced. Yet, such a love can be grown out of such a soil only as it is quickened by the warmth and showers of the Spirit's influence. Natural affections may be the ties that bind into a society unity, individuals, families and tribes; but the love that binds us to God and his Son is *the fruit of the Holy Spirit*. In natures such as ours the love of God is an exotic,—it must not only be planted in our hearts, but also sustained there by the Holy Spirit's *personal care*.

But again, the Holy Spirit is also the dispenser of the Christian's joy, peace and hope in the service of the Christ. Hear the Apostle, as he prays for his brethren at Rome—" Now the God of hope fill you with joy and peace in believing that ye may abound in hope in the power of the Holy Spirit " (Rom. 15 : 13). The same blessed Spirit that quickened the Ephesian believers— the same "Spirit of life in Christ Jesus" which made the Apostle " free from the law of sin and death"—this same Spirit quickens, emancipates and enfranchises every Christian who is made a Son of God.

The eighth of Romans is the Magna Charta of every enfranchised believer who " walks not after the flesh, but after the Spirit." The Apostle insists that "if the Spirit of God dwells in us," that such "*are not in the flesh.*" And while he boldly affirms: "If any man have not the Spirit of Christ, he is none of his"—he as boldly declares that "as many as are led by the Spirit of God, *they* are the Sons of God" (Rom. 8 : 14).

It is not, therefore, by one or two acts good or bad that the Christian is to be judged, but by the consistency and character of his life. "*Enoch walked with God*"—thus our walk must be the evidence to the world that we are led by the Spirit.

There are acts in the lives of unregenerate men and women that are worthy of all commendation. So in the lives of Christians there may be, unfortunately, acts as unchristian as the sin of David or the denial of Peter, or, to quote old Swinnock—"Sheep may fall into the mire; but swine love day and night to wallow in it." Yes, a Christian may stumble and fall, but he is soon up again, and following the leading of the Spirit. His heart temples the Holy Spirit, his life is a redeemed one, and his living will show this as true, nevertheless, that he is dead to the law—that he has been crucified with Christ, and risen with him to that new life which he lives; and "yet no longer I," as Paul says, "but Christ liveth in me, and that life which I now live in the flesh I live in faith—the faith which is in the Son of God, who loved me and gave himself up for me" (Gal. 2 : 20).

One other service of the Holy Spirit to the Christian I linger a moment to simply mention—

After saying that the end of the believer's faith is "the praise of the glory of Christ," the Apostle adds: "In whom having also believed, ye were sealed with the Holy Spirit, which is the earnest of our inheritance unto the redemption of God's own possession, unto the praise of his glory" (Eph. 1: 13, 14). This sealing of the believer, you observe, follows his acceptance of the gospel of salvation.

But the seal of the Spirit is also the earnest of the inheritance which the Christ, by his death, acquired for the believer, or, in other words, is the divine guarantee of its ultimate possession. But in the mean time, by his indwelling power, the Holy Spirit renews, sanctifies, leads, keeps and comforts the heir, thus preparing him *for* that inheritance which Christ has secured to him.

"He that establisheth us with you in Christ," says Paul, "and anointed us, *is God;* who also sealed us, and gave us the earnest of the Spirit in our hearts" (2 Cor. 1: 21, 22). As the preceding sealing was for security, so the preceding "anointing" was for service. If Christians are a *sealed people*, they are also a *devoted people*. As the sealing makes him safe in this inheritance, so the earnest guarantees to him the ultimate realization of the hope he has in Jesus Christ. "For he that hath wrought us for this very thing is God, who gave unto us the earnest of the Spirit" (2 Cor. 5: 5).

However diverse or various may be the gifts of God's people, they have one common origin—"the same Spirit"—or, however different the manifestations of the

Spirit may be to different persons, the end is the same: "*to profit withal.*"

Having thus indicated 1—what the Holy Spirit *is to the Christian,* and 2—what *he does for the Christian,* let us inquire—

III. *What the Christian is to the Holy Spirit.*

From what has been said it is evident that redeemed men and women are not their own, and furthermore, that they are the special subjects of the Holy Spirit's love and guidance. What the Apostle said of the Ephesian believers is just as true of believers now: "Ye are no more strangers and sojourners, but ye are fellow-citizens with the saints and of the household of God, being built upon the foundation of Apostles and prophets, Christ Jesus himself being the chief cornerstone, in whom each several building, fitly framed together, groweth into a holy temple in the Lord; in whom ye also are builded together for a habitation of God in the Spirit" (Eph. 2: 19-22). As believers we are each a part of the household of God, members of the redeemed family; and as such the Holy Spirit evidently regards us. But again—" Know ye not that your bodies are the temple of the Holy Spirit, which is in you, which you have from God? and ye are not your own, for ye were bought with a price; glorify God, therefore, in your body" (1 Cor. 6: 19-20).

Now, in so far as the Holy Spirit appreciates the value of the price paid for our redemption, may we not infer that to that degree will the purchase of that infinite price be precious in his sight? Our acceptance of Christ carries with it not only our devotion to *his* service, but likewise our submission to the love and guidance of the Holy Spirit. If Ananias, who kept back part of the price of his land, "lied unto the Holy Spirit," what shall be thought of the sin of him who, having devoted himself and all he has to God, takes it back in part or in whole, that he may, as James says, "spend it in his pleasures?" Brethren, when we call to mind the fact that as believers we are "the epistles of Christ, written not with ink, but with the Spirit of the living God" (2 Cor. 3: 3), "What manner of persons ought we to be in all holy living and godliness?" (2 Peter 3: 11).

In closing, allow mention to be made of some lessons suggested by this imperfect discussion.

1. Every visitation of the Holy Spirit and every gift of his grace should be prayerfully cherished and encouraged.

"That good thing which was committed unto thee, guard through the Holy Spirit which dwelleth in us" (2 Tim. 1: 14). "Stir up the gift of God, which is in thee, by the laying on of my hands" (2 Tim. 1: 6). If such exhortations were appropriate to Timothy, surely we ought to take heed to this grace which has been bestowed upon us also. And even more appropriate to us, and to our times, certainly, are these words of Paul to his "Son in the gospel," that breathe for his welfare a concern so affectionate and earnest: "O Timothy, guard that which is committed to thee, turning away from the profane babblings and oppositions of the knowledge which is falsely so called; which some professing have erred concerning the faith" (1 Tim. 6: 20, 21).

2. If we would be *guided by the Holy Spirit,* we must "*walk in the Spirit,*" and to do this we must "*live in the Spirit.*"

Such a life is inseparable from conflict: "For the flesh lusteth against the Spirit and the Spirit against the flesh." It is impossible that it be otherwise, "for these" (*i.e.,* the flesh and the Spirit) "are contrary the one to the other" (Gal. 5:7). We can choose which of these two lives shall be ours, and we must choose and we *do choose*—we can't live both lives. Alas, that so few find and so many seem not to learn that conformity to the world is rebellion against the Holy Spirit! Alas for Christianity that more Christians are not transformed (or literally), transfigured by the Holy Spirit's indwelling! Say what we will, the love of the world and the pride of life and the lusts of the flesh will be cast out of us only as we are "filled with the Spirit."

3. Let us understand our duties to the Holy Spirit and faithfully perform them as in the fear of God. "Grieve not the Holy Spirit of God, in whom ye were sealed unto the day of redemption" (Eph. 4: 30). Need I say that these words of caution and command demand our most prayerful and constant attention?

We need the use of no pessimistic spectacles to see in our own lives, and in the lives of many Christians about us, too much that *must* and *does* grieve the Holy Spirit of God. Nor would I be overstating a truth which, doubtless, they feel most deeply who live most closely to God, were I to add, that until the living of Christians is more fully submitted to the leading of the Holy Spirit we shall look and labor in vain for such a revival in the churches as our needs demand. Let us remember these words, "God hath called us not for uncleanness, but in sanctification; therefore, he that rejecteth, rejecteth not man, but God" (1 Thess. 4: 7, 8). Sins, even in Christians, may change their dress and their names, and yet be just as hateful to God. Under the deception of "prudent economy" we may disguise a covetousness as odious in God's sight as the grossest idolatry. Under the masks of business, or social duties, we may hide a worldliness as despicable as paganism. And under the pretence of church benevolence we may bring into the church of God entertainments that wound our Lord in the house of his friends. Before the Holy Spirit can fill us, or our churches, much must be scourged from the temples of our hearts and sanctuaries. It is not the *kind* of sin that grieves the Holy Spirit; sin of *any kind* must grieve him who is himself the essence of holiness.

Again, we are warned: "Quench not the Spirit" (1 Thess. 5: 19). As the fire on the altar may be so neglected and covered up as to be left to smoulder amid ashes that hide its heat and light, so may we quench the Holy Spirit in our hearts. "Whatever," said Dr. C. S. Robinson, "the Holy Spirit prompts a true Christian to do for the glory of God, he *allures* him to do in a modest way, and with a disposition of indescribable tenderness." Mackay makes this distinction, "*Resist*" is the word applied to the unconverted; "*Grieve*" is that applied to the individual Christian; "*Quench*" is that which has reference to the saints when gathered together waiting on the Spirit. This may be correct; and yet the individual may *quench* the presence of the Holy Spirit in his soul by his neglect and sins, as well as *grieve* him by such things.

The warning of the Apostolic Seer has long since become history. Looking back from these "latter days," we painfully realize the truth of what he said to Timothy: "The Spirit saith *expressly* that in the latter times some shall fall away from the faith, giving heed to seducing spirits and doctrines of demons, through the hypocrisy of men that speak lies; branded in their own consciences as with a hot iron; forbidding to marry, and commanding to abstain from meats which God created to be received with thanksgiving by them that believe and know the truth" (1 Tim. 4:1-3.) The word of God not only thus smites the pretensions of spiritualism and the presumptions of Romanism, but, at the same time, exposes the open and disguised designs of many another tendency of our times to oppose or corrupt "the faith" which was "once for all delivered unto the saints." Let us not forget that we are to contend for and defend "the faith of Jesus," but in doing so let us also remember that, after all, the best possible defence that can be made is being made by those whose lives most closely imitate the life of Jesus Christ our Lord. The tongue of the Christian and of the Church is still the old and unanswerable "*tongue of flame.*"

"If ye then were raised together with Christ, seek the things that are above, where Christ is seated at the right hand of God: set your affections on things that are above; not on the things that are upon the earth. For *ye died* and your life is hid with Christ in God" (Col. 3: 1–3). And "insomuch as you are partakers of Christ's sufferings, rejoice; that at the revelation of his glory, also, ye may rejoice with *exceeding* joy. If ye are reproached for the name of Christ blessed are ye; because the Spirit of glory and the Spirit of God resteth upon you" (1 Pet. 4: 13, 14).

On the day of Pentecost, said William Arthur: "Christianity faced the world—a new religion, without a history, without a priesthood, a college, without a people—without a portion; . . . her tongue of fire was her sole instrument of aggression." But, my brethren, how is it now? Now, besides having the complete canon of God's inspired word, we have almost everything else except "*the tongue of fire.*" This inspired word needs inspired men to preach it. The churches need the old pentecostal power for worship and witness, and the energy of the Holy Spirit to make her methods of work effective. Believers need the Holy Spirit, enshrined in the indwelling word, abiding in them, that the divine word, aflame with the light and life of the Holy Spirit, may transfigure them, and, through them, quicken from the death of sin to eternal life them that are lost.

Finally, brethren: "The grace of our Lord Jesus Jesus Christ and the love of God and the communion of the Holy Spirit be with you all." Amen.

XIII.

THE SPIRIT OF PROPHECY.

BY BISHOP W. R. NICHOLSON, D.D.

THE subject assigned me is The Spirit of Prophecy. Shall we take this to mean the characteristic qualities of prophecy, as when we speak of the spirit of a book? Or shall we understand that the Holy Spirit is meant? Practically what is the difference? If we investigate the characteristics of prophecy, it is no other than the work of the Holy Spirit we shall be considering, since he, the author of prophecy, has made it just what it is. On the other hand, if we fix attention directly on the Holy Spirit as self-revealed in prophecy, the qualities of his work therein are what must be examined. The difference is not material. Forasmuch, however, as the object in view of this conference is to identify, venerate and glorify the Holy Spirit, I shall interpret our subject as if it read, The Holy Spirit as he is in Prophecy.

Prophecy, as here used, must have the meaning it bears in common parlance—predictive prophecy. Since, if not thus restricted, it includes every subject in the Bible; the prophets having been teachers of the whole revealed will of God. With closer accuracy, then, we read our subject thus, The Holy Spirit as he is in Predictive Prophecy.

I shall not stop to prove that the predictions of the Bible are genuine miraculous previsions of the future. The wealth of proof on that point no drafts of infidelity can diminish. That truth I assume and lay down as a postulate. Neither shall I waste our time in adducing proof of the Holy Spirit being the author of those predictions. The Bible, with authority, ascribes them to him, and common sense decides that no human sagacity could so have foreseen the future. This also we start from as a postulate.

And now with the miraculous predictions of the Spirit before us, our concern is reverently to study him therein; learning something of his prophetic revelations and of our consequent obligations, and how we may become yet more enriched in Christian experience.

In the first place, the Holy Spirit in prophecy means that we shall understand him.

This remark has much the look of a truism; for why, otherwise, should he speak to us at all? But it has been called in question. It is the key to our subject; and certainly, for the honor of the Holy Spirit, we are in duty bound to settle this question one way or the other.

The Spirit in prophecy means to be understood. Some difficulties there are, of course, in the interpreting of prophecy. We cannot always make sure of a particular application, nor of a particular chronological relation. But we can make sure, almost without exception, of the main fact predicted. And is it not just the same as regards the Gospel itself? That "by one man sin entered into the world, and death by sin, and so death passed upon all men, for that all sinned," is a plain statement of fact, and we receive it; but is there nothing in it that is not understood? Who can thoroughly explain the Federal Headship of Adam? That Jesus Christ "bore our sins in his own body," and made expiation of sin, is a declaration clear as light, and we receive it; but is there nothing in it that is not understood? Who can convert into a sunbeam the inscrutable philosophy of the Federal Headship of the Second Adam? And also here and there in non-prophetic Scripture are there not even statements that are confessedly obscure? But who is so presumptuous as to turn rare difficulties into universal objections, and thence to infer that all Scripture is not understandable? Let prophecy be fairly dealt with. If there be the devoutly desirous mind, if pains be taken to ascertain the grammatical common sense of words and sentences, and to compare Scripture with Scripture, if there be patience, and perseverance, and the prostration of the will at the feet of God's will, then one shall as surely know, in the main, the prophetic mind of the Spirit, as that the Spirit has so expressed his mind at all. All this, however, is no more than the Gospel itself requires in order to its being understood.

As in the Gospel, so in prophecy, the Spirit speaks

on purpose to be understood. He himself describes it as "a lamp shining in a dark place;" but what sort of a light is that by which we cannot see? He calls it "a sure word of prophecy:" but how do words assure us if they give us not their meaning? "Ye do well," he says, "that ye take heed to it:" but how can we heed what we cannot think of? The Holy Spirit even shows us that his own honor is involved in our being able to understand his predictions: no prophecy, says he, ever came by the will of man, but men spake from God, being moved by the Holy Ghost, and therefore it is that prophecy is as a light in a dark place—that is, is not a darkening of counsel by words without knowledge (2 Pet. 1 : 19–21). He expressly tells us the purpose of predictive prophecy: "to show to his servants the things which must come to pass" (Rev. 1 : 1); but what kind of a showing is that which does not show at all? He pronounces a special blessing upon those "who read and hear the words of the prophecy, and keep the things which are written therein" (Rev. 1 : 3); but how can he bless our reading and hearing what we cannot know, and how shall we keep what we have not got? So obvious is it that the Spirit's predictions are a reflection of his own mind to our minds, and that his use of prophetic language is fraught with a Divine frankness and perspicuity.

Moreover, his providence in the past is a historic demonstration. Refer to any prophecy fulfilled. Lay alongside the 28th chapter of Deuteronomy the history of the Jews 1500 years afterwards, more than 3000 years afterwards, and did ever mirror give back more accurately the face of the beholder, than the actual sufferings of that people the very words of the Spirit in their plain grammatical sense? He called Cyrus by name more than 150 years before his birth, and said that he would open before him the gates of brass, and cut in sunder the bars of iron, that he might deliver the elect people from Babylon, and say to Jerusalem, Thou shalt be built, and to the temple, Thy foundation shall be laid; and did not the identical Cyrus appear on the stage of action at the proper time, and were not the things foretold done to the very letter? When, in words so many, in oracles so lofty, all along the ages so vast, the Spirit had pre-written the life and doings of Messiah, did ever pen of history record more exactly events of the past than pen of prediction events of the future? Even the least events were minutely measured by the words of prediction, and were such an answer to the words as is a river to each little crook in the channel; the thirty pieces of silver, the spitting, the scourging, the thirst, the vinegar, and all the rest, being as strictly in occurrence as they had been in prediction. Statements, too, that might well have seemed inadvertences in the use of words—as that Messiah should die as a malefactor and a slave, an object of hatred, a butt of ridicule, and yet that he should have honorable burial —were accomplished in every word. And, O wonderful! the Virgin Motherhood—did that prediction mean just what it expressed? A virgin mother! Impossible. Against all experience, against creation's laws. And learned conceit wags its head, mouthing the criticism, Figurative, Mystical. Ah, but the Holy Spirit had said it, and in the simplest, frankest way possible; and when, 700 years afterwards, the time had come, a virgin mother Mary WAS. Can demonstration go further, that the Spirit means us to interpret his predictions according to the established usage of language?

But you say, There are figures of speech in prophecy. Yes, and do not yourselves abound in the use of figures? Are they not the current speech of daily life? When the Holy Spirit predicted that the future Messiah would say, "Many bulls have compassed Me," "Dogs have compassed Me," are not the figures instantly detected and clearly interpreted? When Cyrus is represented as addressing Jerusalem and the temple, is not the meaning self-evident? And if, in any instance, it be doubtful whether there be a figure, a patient examination of the connection will generally be satisfactory.

But you say, the symbols of prophecy—they at least are riddles insolvable. Well, look at the Colossus of Daniel—the metallic image. The prophecy itself interprets it. And so it is with many symbols. When, however, symbols are left unexplained, not seldom a comparison of Scripture with Scripture will make them plain; the symbolic interpretations given, so many and various, being examples of interpretation, and, besides, what is foreshown in symbol being foretold in other forms elsewhere. Patience, perseverance and humility will rarely fail to bring you in contact with the essential fact in the symbol, and advance your instruction in righteousness.

And now shall we embrace that obnoxious dictum, that unfulfilled prophecy can be understood, even in the main, only after the fulfillment? Does the Holy Spirit say so? Where? Just the contrary, as we have seen. It is expressly unfulfilled prophecy that he characterizes as a lamp shining in a dark place; that he declares to be for the purpose of showing his servants things to come. Nor is there a single accomplished prediction whose words have not been grammatically realized. Only take the terms of prophecy in their obvious sense, and you cannot but rightly anticipate the events, although the fulfillment is ahead of you.

When we read, Thus saith the Lord God, Behold, I will put the tribes of Ephraim with Judah, and will gather the children of Israel from among the nations whither they have gone, and will bring them into their own land, and make them one nation in the land, and they shall walk in My judgments, and shall dwell in the land that I gave to Jacob, wherein their fathers dwelt, they and their children and their children's children forever, yea, I will be their God and they shall be My people, and My sanctuary shall be in the midst of them forevermore (Ezek. 37); do not the words absolutely shut off all interpretations save one? When God said to David, I will make thee a house, and thine house and thy kingdom shall be established forever (2 Sam. 7), I will not lie to David (Ps. 89), I will set up thy seed after thee, which shall proceed out of thy bowels, and I will establish his kingdom and the throne of his kingdom forever (2 Sam. 7), of the increase of his government and peace no end upon the throne of David and upon his kingdom, to order it, and to establish it with judgment and justice even forever (Isa. 9); are not the words a very sunshine in their clearness? And when the Spirit lets us hear the angel Gabriel assuring Mary that her virgin-born should have the throne of his father David (Luke 1), and writes for us two genealogies of Jesus, whose united testimony is a redundancy of proof that he is that offspring of David to whom was bequeathed David's kingdom, and when the Spirit adds that Jesus is as a nobleman gone into a far country to receive for himself a kingdom and to return, and that upon his return he will build again the tabernacle of David, which is fallen down, and that the Son of man, having come in his glory, shall then sit upon the throne of his glory (Luke 19); Matt. 25; Acts 15; is there a human intelligence that does not instantly see what these communications naturally and irrepressibly mean? And by the fact of the literal fulfillment of every predicted circumstance of Messiah's first coming, does not the Holy Spirit protest against the taking in a non-natural sense what he says of the kingdom to be set up at Messiah's second coming? It is David's throne, David's kingdom, the Christ is to occupy. This does not refer to Christ's blessed reign in our hearts, for never did David so reign; nor to the Son of God's reign in the third heaven, for never did David so reign. The language of the prediction demands that he, the virgin-born, whose name is The Mighty God, shall visibly reign on the earth as David's lineal successor, only incomparably more gloriously; that he shall reign as a man, yet in his majesty as God, with judgment and justice, in purity and holiness, in love and blessedness.

When we read that there shall be a new earth and a new atmosphere (2 Pet. 3), so glorious that the former, the present visible creation, shall not be remembered nor come into mind (Isa. 65: 17); that there shall still be nations dwelling on the earth after the stupendous conflagration foretold by Isaiah and Peter; that the fire shall be for perdition of ungodly men, which perdition shall be inflicted upon certain multitudes, while yet there shall be those that escape (Isa. 66: 19); that the risen saints, having returned with their Lord, shall be associated with him as kings and priests for the benefit of the nations, and with him shall rule the nations (Rev. 1: 6; 2: 26; 3: 21); that the animal creation shall be so adapted to the new earth, wherein dwelleth righteousness, the wolf shall dwell with the lamb, and the lion shall eat straw like the ox (Isa. 11) —can you imagine a greater explicitness of statement? Does the Spirit not speak as meaning to be understood?

But you say. I have always thought of that tremendous conflagration as sweeping away from the earth all the inhabitants. Whence, then, did you get the thought? Not from what the Spirit tells you; for he declares the very opposite.

But you continue, It is absurd to construe literally the statement that the lion shall eat straw like the ox; it is contradictory of the lion's nature. Well, if it is figurative, what does the figure signify? To find out this were like hunting for the lost pleiad, and would require the telescopic vision of a superhuman mind. Against the lion's nature? Yes, and it is against the nature of a virgin to bear a son; but the Holy Spirit once said that so it should be, and so it was.

But you say again, What mistakes students of prophecy are constantly making with regard to the date of the Lord's coming. Have their mistakes come, then, from simply being guided by the words of the Spirit? On the contrary, his express words are, "It is not for you to know the times and the seasons, which the Father hath put in his own power." Signs of the coming are given us, but the date is hidden. Comparatively few, however, are the students of prophecy who are so unwarrantably betrayed into such mistakes.

In fine, the Spirit's expressed purpose is to show us things to come. His predictions are obvious ideas, for he bids us give heed to them. His predictions are light, for so he names them. His predictions are grammatically simple and clear, for so his providence has demonstrated them. If, then, we have no interest in prophecy, we dishonor the Holy Spirit. If we take no pains to understand what he has been at so much pains to cause us to understand, we fail so far forth to put ourselves in communication with him. And, saith the Lord, "Them that honor Me I will honor."

The intelligible mind of the Spirit is the spirit of prophecy.

In the second place, the Holy Spirit in prophecy gives us a great deal to understand.

In fact he crowds the Bible with his prophetic communications. And, by the way, the abundance of them is further confirmation of their explicitness; for why should they be so immensely many, if, for the most part, we cannot understand them? Does the Spirit pleasure himself at puzzling us with enigmas?—a cynical pleasure long drawn out. But to the point before us.

Certainly he is graciously revealed in his other teachings. His adorable relations in the Godhead—his office as the Comforter—his ministration of salvation to individual souls, in all this he is the very and wonderful love of God. And yet to himself all this has not seemed to be enough. He would instruct us as to the future, and more and more enrich us with his own thoughts and purposes. And that his prophecies are so very many, illustrates how important to us he regards them as being.

The proportion of prophecy in the Bible is enormous. Excluding the merely historical parts, the predictions occupy perhaps two-thirds of Scripture; and if also we exclude the predictions that have been fulfilled, those yet to be fulfilled are, as to the remainder of Scripture in preponderating proportion. Now this is a remarkable status of the Word of God. We might have argued that the truths of personal salvation must have the precedence in amount of space. On the contrary, the Holy Spirit has argued that saving truth is as the foundation, prophetic truth as the superstructure; that the constituent parts of a superstructure, like the bricks in a building, are to the stones of the foundation as many to one; and that just as a foundation without its superstructure serves not its purpose, so saving truth without the prophetic truth is in an imperfect condition, being detached from its proper development. The exceeding proportion of prophecy in Scripture, then, is a most instructive fact. What stores of sacred learning the Spirit has thus been treasuring up for us! So that if it seem not to us that, for our highest Christian well-being, we are dependent, in no small degree, on so large an array of Scripture, we are no less than at war with the mind of the Spirit.

What variety of subjects, too, within this wide range of unfulfilled prophecy! Nations, empires, individuals; judgments, blessings, glory; doctrines, experiences; the dappled history of the Church along this dispensation; the restoration of Israel; the great apostasy with its truculent aspect; the rise, character, development, and overthrow of the imperial Antichrist; the Christ as coming again, his Epiphany and Parousia; the judgment of the nations, the judgment of Christendom; the

First Resurrection; the risen saints joint kings and priests with their Lord; the kingdom established, the throne of the great King earth's central splendor; the supreme effusion of the Holy Spirit; earth's renewal, the world's millennial blessedness; the final outbreak of rebellion, the final subjugation, the sudden, complete, everlasting eradication of evil; the kingdom of the Christ, the kingdom of God, the kingdom of heaven, one kingdom, in unquestioned sovereignty; the tabernacle of God on earth, God dwelling with men, no more death, neither sorrow, nor any more pain. An immensity of interests. Momentous subjects all. Verily a vast deal concerning the future the Spirit has given us to understand.

Now wherefore? Because in this fore-written history of the times to come, our own personal interests, as Christians, are illustrated and enforced. Our souls are touched on every side.

Our knowledge is increased; not a vague generality of knowledge, like as that we shall be happy hereafter, but knowledge made up of many facts, bristling all over with salient points; and knowledge is power.

Our historic instinct is gratified; for as in the history of the past we have an intellectual pleasure in noticing how the principles of human action, as exemplified in events, have been characterized as good or bad, so in this predictive history of the future, what high mental satisfaction in observing the consummate results of the very principles now at work and influencing mankind.

We see that ultimate is the consecutiveness of sin and perdition, of godliness and glory; and we expand into the sublime thought, that God's universe is one organic whole in the interest of truth, and law, and justice, and righteousness, and love.

Our feelings with regard to the great hereafter are illumined, stimulated, intensified; for as, like a panorama, these tremendous events are acting before us in prophetic vision, the greatness of the scenes is thrown back upon ourselves, for we shall be there, and we are lifted into the majesty of conviction, and the glow of self-respect. Meanwhile all present things take on a subdued look, the world's businesses, excitements, and friendships lie low, comparatively, in our estimation. We are breathing a purer air.

Our trust in God's providence is quickened and enlarged; for in these ultimate events, as being the harvest of the ages, we see how minute must be now his observation of men, and yet how all-comprehending the sweep of his plan, and we warm into acquiescence in the present sovereign control of affairs.

Our appreciation of the whole Bible is promoted; for even its non-prophetic revelations, in the light of this predicted future, shoot forth into charming display. This effect was produced by certain predictions already accomplished: there, for instance, was God's revelation of the Levitical Ritual; it was prediction that vindicated the Divine wisdom therein, and made consummate both priest and victim in him who should be wounded for our transgressions. And so as to predictions yet to be accomplished. How poor were the significance of Israel's calling as a peculiar people, except for prediction exalting them into the children of the Better Covenant, into the radiating centre of the world's salvation, into a predominant position among the peoples of the ages to come! What, to us, were the value of God's revelation, that David should be king, did not prediction reveal his appointment therein to be type and earnest of the Messianic King? That the blood of Jesus Christ cleanseth from all sin is a most gracious revelation; but it is prediction that designates the far-reaching magnificent consequences of that cleansing, making the grandeur of result answer back to the grandeur of cause (the atonement), and lighting up the truth with a noontide of splendor. That the believer is one with Christ, as the branch with the vine, is a Divine assurance most grateful; but prediction is the arithmetic of its preciousness, and sums it up in a far more exceeding and eternal wealth of glory

Yes, the Blessed Holy Spirit has good reasons for the abundance of his predictions. He knows our needs, and his benevolent mind sympathizes with us. No wonder that his prophecies loom within the Bible horizon in Alpine proportions. No wonder that from Genesis to Apocalypse they stud the expanse of revelation like stars in the sky, and make of the Bible a luminous whole. No wonder that here and there, again and again, they shine like the sun in the heavens, turning night into day, melting winter into summer, vivifying truth with foliage and color and fruit. No wonder that out of the bubbling spring of the Protevangelium—the woman's promised seed—on and on, all the way to the gorgeous vision of the New Jerusalem, they have flowed like a fertilizing Nile, meeting indeed in their course with many a cataract of calamity foretold, but watering the deserts of human thought, and causing sorrowing souls to blossom like the rose.

If, then, we turn away from earnest, humble, patient, devout study of prophecy, slighting the wonderful things which the Spirit has given us to understand, substituting therefor our own guesses and worldly prejudices, are we not contemning his wisdom, are we not grieving his love? And if we find ourselves bemoaning a lack of spiritual power, and that our churches, like the fig tree in Gospel story, while putting forth leaves of outward prosperity, are yet without fruit, would the cause be far to seek? For if the Bible of the Spirit is a lamp to our feet, the prophecies of the Spirit are the brightness of its flame; if the Bible of the Spirit is a tower into which the righteous runneth and is safe, the prophecies of the Spirit are at once the massiveness and the loftiness of the tower.

The instructive mind of the Spirit is the spirit of prophecy.

Thirdly, the Holy Spirit in prophecy is pre-eminently a witness for Christ.

It is his own declaration that "the testimony of Jesus is the spirit of prophecy." He does indeed bear witness to Christ in the non-prophetic Scriptures; as in the law of God, in the truth of the Atonement, in justification by faith, and otherwise.

In the prophetic Scriptures, however, not only is all this essentially included, but the Christly testimony is more; more in bulk, since the predictions are so numerous, more in completeness, since the predictions are the unfolding of the final issue. For what were salvation without its consummation? Somewhat of a torso —a decapitated blessing; a present good, yet partial, because without a delineated future. The Christ is but defectively revealed, except he is seen in the advancing final results of his work.

A prophetic witness to Christ the Holy Spirit has been from the beginning. Doubly so in the Old Testament, wherein his predictions embraced both comings of Christ; singly so in the New Testament, wherein his predictions are limited to the returning Christ; but wherein, in attitude intent, and with index finger, he is evermore pointing us onward to the Christly glories, and with voice urging us to utmost devotion in hastening the day of God. His predictive testimony to Jesus is what the Spirit loves to maintain.

The Gospel of Jesus is the Gospel of the Spirit. But the Gospel of Jesus is the Gospel of the kingdom; for he told his disciples that to preach the kingdom of God was that for which he was sent (Luke 4 : 43), and accordingly, as it is said, he did go everywhere preaching the Gospel of the kingdom (Matthew 4: 23). Now what Jesus preached the Spirit preaches, for he had the Spirit without measure. The Gospel of the Spirit is the Gospel of the kingdom. It was the delight of Jesus' heart, it is the delight of the Spirit's heart.

What, then, is the Gospel of the kingdom? The Gospel of repentance, faith, forgiveness, acceptance, eternal life, is not that it? Yes, but also it is more. Personal salvation from sin, reconciliation with God, is indeed essential to one's entrance into the kingdom; for the kingdom, in the person of the great King, is grounded on his redemptive sufferings and priestly functions. But just as the Saviour's expiation of sin is itself not the kingdom, so the believer's personal salvation is itself not the same as his investiture with the kingdom. Every saved man is sure of the kingdom; but his being saved and his having the kingdom, while linked together as cause and effect, are two distinct things. The Gospel of the kingdom is the good tidings of the kingdom; and while in those good tidings is included the Gospel of salvation by faith in the atoning Saviour, they are also our assurance of the perfection of that Gospel; they are the ultimate expression of the efficacy of redemption, the fulness of the Spirit's statement of salvation, the glory of the Saviour at the highest point of conception.

This is what the Spirit in prophecy is so actively engaged in testifying of Christ. He works to lift our eyes up and away from that inadequate view of the Saviour, that the church is his kingdom. Instead, he fastens attention to the nobleman's return from the far country, bringing his kingdom with him, as the transcendent expression of Christ. He commemorates to us the Thessalonian believers, who, having "turned to God from idols to serve the living and true God," did then complete their Christian position by taking the attitude of "waiting for his Son from heaven." Thus two-fold is the purpose of his predictive testimony to Christ: first, to teach us, and prompt us to, a yet greater and worthier honoring of the Saviour, both as to the efficacy of his saving work and as to the final consummation of his triumph as Saviour ; and secondly, thereby to bring us into a more complete expression of experience and character. Hence the pains the Spirit is at to make the Gospel of the kingdom attractive; sketching that scene of royalty in such colors as to the appreciative eye are vivid realizations; representing the King in his beauty, around him the risen saints crowned and enthroned, earth at her jubilee, holiness ruling the world, and Jesus, the Lamb of God, the glory of it all.

Not to study the Spirit in prophecy, therefore, is so far forth not to study Christ. Nor are we fully in communion with the Spirit, if, in defiance of his teachings, we are yielding to that worldly notion, so prevalent in the church, of social progress gradually dissolving in universal blessedness, and so we are not yearning for and expecting that Epiphany from heaven, the miraculous introduction into the earth of the kingdom of God. Oh, there is a thrilling sense of redemption in the prophecies. When Jesus, in the way to Emmaus, expounded the predictions concerning himself, the hearts of the disciples burned within them; and when the Holy Spirit, whose own was the burning power of those words of Jesus, speaks to us of that same Jesus in the sublime oracles of the future, what a blaze of power should be in our hearts!

The Christly mind of the Spirit is the spirit of prophecy.

Fourthly, the Holy Spirit in prophecy glorifies himself.

It is the prerogative of Deity to make a display of the Divine glory. As the Father asserts his Eternal Majesty, and the Son, while yet in submission to his Filial relation, asserts his equality with the Father, so the Third Person of the adorable Trinity, while yet in submission to his Processional relation, asserts his equality with both the Father and the Son. Not otherwise could the Eternal Three in One enter into communication with men; and it were a forfeiture of the Divine character of the Spirit's revelations, if he himself were hidden in them out of sight. It is what we should have anticipated, then, that his sublime oracles of the future would have upon them the impress of his own Personal glory.

We find, accordingly, that he does assert himself in prophecy with a surpassing solemnity. "The blasphemy against the Spirit shall not be forgiven. Whosoever shall speak against the Holy Spirit shall not be forgiven, neither in this age, nor in that which is to come." This warning was spoken by the Lord Jesus in honor of the Holy Spirit, but the Spirit himself inspired the evangelist to write it. Now there is a prediction in it; for in addition to its being said, that the man committing that sin shall never be forgiven, either in this age or in the age to come, it is of course implied that if there shall be one committing that sin in the age to come (and the Scripture is express that there will be more or less of sin in the millennial age), he shall not be forgiven. So much of a prophetic word is in it, and it is the Spirit's solemn assertion, in connection with the age to come, of his own Eternal Majesty, his adorable sacredness, and of how indispensable, in the salvation of men, his power shall continue to be.

But he further asserts it with a surpassing sublimity. What wonderful works of grace he prophetically ascribes to himself. True, every word of the present salvation is the Spirit's self-assertion of his glory; but nowhere else, as in the Gospel of the kingdom, is his self-assertion so glorious. What a wonder it were, if a whole nation, without the exception of a single individual, were converted to God. But that very marvel of Almighty power and grace is no dream. His own predictions claim that he will pour upon the seed of Israel the spirit of grace and supplication, and they shall look on him whom they pierced, and shall mourn as one mourneth for an only son (Zech. 12: 10); and he will put his law in their inward parts and write it in their hearts, and none shall say to another, know the Lord, for they shall know him from the least of them to the greatest of them, and their iniquity shall be forgiven, and their sin be remembered no more (Jer. 31: 33, 34); and they shall inherit the land forever, the branch of his planting, the work of his hands, that he may be glorified (Isa. 60: 21). Yet what is a whole nation's conversion to God, as compared with that of a world?—when Israel's light shall flood the globe, and kings shall come to the brightness of her rising (Isa. 60), and all peoples, made willing in the day of his power, shall remember and turn to the Lord, the skies pouring down righteousness, salvation growing up from the earth, the effect of righteousness, quietness and assurance forever (Ps. 22: 27; Isa. 45: 8; 32: 17). Nor is this all. For as once the Spirit moved upon the dark face of the deep, and there was light, so, his predictions assure us, he will again move upon what he calls this groaning creation; and at his touch, "the mountains skipping like rams, and the little hills like lambs," all things shall become readjusted, creation's groans be hushed, earth appear in a new garniture of beauty, beasts of the field and fowls of heaven and creeping things of the ground transformed, neither carnivorous beast nor poisonous creature desecrating God's world for evermore, and we, though now so opaque in person and character, shall brighten over the laughing earth into a light like unto a stone most precious, even like a jasper stone, clear as crystal (Rom. 8; Hos. 2; Isa. 11; Rev. 21).

Now what transcendent works of the Spirit. Topmost achievements of his grace and power. And has he told us of them without designing to win us into a larger appreciation of his preciousness to us, and thereby to promote our worshipful reverence of him? These prophetic splendors, as though a mere background, do but project into view the seraphic intensity of the trinal ascription, Holy, Holy, Holy!

The adorable mind of the Spirit is the spirit of prophecy.

Fifthly, the Holy Spirit in prophecy is the minister of righteousness.

As in precept, doctrine, exhortation, so in prediction, his purpose is to draw us away from sin, and advance us in righteous living. The one pervading theme of his prophecies is Christ; every one of them, if not directly, then indirectly, referring to him. And what but Christ is the power of righteousness? Any event seen to be connected with him, even if distantly, is a stream of holy influence; just as the woman felt his health-giving virtue while yet touching but the hem of his garment. Read the harrowing prophecy, still in process of fulfillment, of the calamities of the Jews, and does not the cheek tingle at that continuous doom of unchristianness? Witness the prophecy of the Four

Great Monarchies, and while you see beforehand that gigantic image ground to powder, and are in the midst of the confused dust of gold and silver and brass and iron and clay, you stand aghast at the devouring jealousy of a Holy God when Christ is rejected.

But in his direct prophecies of Christ how signally the Spirit serves the cause of righteousness. Forewarning us of yet fiercer conflicts with the world-rulers of this darkness, the spiritual armies of wickedness, he averts unhappy forebodings, and magnifies the free grace of the Gospel as the power for service, by assuring us that the great dragon, the old serpent, called the Devil and Satan, the people of God shall overcome by the blood of the Lamb and by the word of their testimony. Picturing the peeled and suffering Jews looking upon him whom they pierced, he makes us see that they become all righteous by the blood that cleanseth. Arraying before us the Ancient of days sitting, his garment white as snow, the hair of his head like pure wool, his throne fiery flames, his wheels burning fire, he shows us the Son of man coming, coming to the Ancient of days, coming with the clouds of heaven, giving the wicked nations to the burning flame, receiving dominion and glory and a kingdom, that all peoples and languages should serve him; and we turn with horror from the atheistic sentiments now so threatening among the nations, and clasp the faith of Christ as our only refuge from ungodliness and anarchy and perdition. He writes down for us that word of Jesus, "Behold, I come quickly," and associates with it the prophecy: "He that is unrighteous, let him do unrighteousness still, and he that is filthy, let him be made filthy still, and he that is righteous, let him do righteousness still;" and we see that character at the last is a fixture, projecting itself into the eternal state, and we think of the only force that betimes can revolutionize character—the blood that takes away sin, the faith in Christ that works by love.

Moreover, what express emphasis the Spirit puts upon prophecy in its bearing on a holy life. Does he warn against the loss of the soul? "The Son of man shall come in the glory of his Father with his angels." Does he speak of subduing the lusts of the flesh? "When Christ, your life, shall appear, then shall ye also appear with him in glory." Does he command sobriety of life? "Yourselves know perfectly that the day of the Lord so cometh as a thief in the night." Does he exhort us to patience in the midst of sufferings? "The coming of the Lord draweth nigh." In fine, would he have us deny ungodliness and worldly lusts, and live soberly, righteously and godly in this present world? "Looking for that blessed hope, and the glorious appearing of the great God and our Saviour Jesus Christ."

Now the predominant sin of the church is love of the world. It invades our thoughts, supplies our motives, captivates our affections, damages our religious service; rules in our families, is the keynote of our social arrangements; deadens the spirituality of deacons, elders and vestrymen, poisons the meditations of the preacher, robs the sermon of its unction, shuts off the congregation from the demonstration of the Spirit and of power. Against it the Spirit warns. But precept and exhortation are not enough. We need vividness of impression. We need to SEE the working out of worldly principles and methods. It is the Spirit's prophecies that supply this need. His brilliant coloring of the world's approaching catastrophe, his panorama of the final disasters of our boasted civilization, his startling prevision of the miraculousness of the introduction of God's kingdom into the earth—these are the teachings that break the spell of the enchanter, and for the sleepiness of mere hearsay substitute the very sight of the roaring lion of the tribe of Judah. Worldliness cannot live in the prophetic fires of the Second Coming.

Thus is it that prophecy is pre-eminently the ministry of righteousness. And it is largely because of the neglect of it, largely because the Spirit's fore-written history of events to come is unstudied, unthought of, unknown, that Christians' lives are so far away from Gospel living, and the churches are cold and formal.

The holy mind of the Spirit is the spirit of prophecy.

In the next place, the Holy Spirit in prophecy is the Minister of joy.

Certainly he is the Spirit of joy outside the prophecies. But all the joy of present salvation is not sufficient for our wants. So the Spirit himself has decided, since, by reason of his itemized predictions, he multiplies the joy. Certainly we can trust God, though we see not a step before us. Yet knowledge is good. The specifying of one's blessednesses is an enhancement of the blessedness. Hence the size of the Bible; including so many things solely for the purpose of amplifying our sensibilities.

One joy of prophecy is that of knowing God's plan as to the varying fortunes of the Gospel. What are now the Gospel's circumstances in Christendom? With an eye to its spiritual power, do we see it in the ascendant? The facts are the other way. Multiform denials of the faith. The very basic elements of salvation rejected, contemned, ridiculed, even in high places of the professing church itself. The disproportion in Christendom as regards a personal profession of the Gospel enormous. Certainly there are more true Christians in the world to-day than ever before; but also there are more people in the world than ever before, and the disproportion is as huge as ever. And as regards the minority making the profession the ratio of spiritual reality to unreality microscopic; a minority within a minority. A tiny lump of sugar in a gallon of coffee. And has it not always been so? The three thousand at Pentecost, in itself a magnificent triumph, was but a minim out of the myriads in Jerusalem that day. And to-day more than a billion of mankind know nothing of the saving virtue of the Lord Jesus. Whence is our comfort as regards the destiny of the Gospel? If you point to Japan, and say, Behold, a mighty nation getting ready to proclaim Christianity as the national religion, at once the bluff fact strikes us in the face that they are fascinated by the material prosperity of Christendom; and obtrusive is the inference, as is that of a theorem in geometry, that, having nationally adopted Christianity, they will only have become like the other so-called Christian nations. Or if you say, In spite of this outlook, we have the word of our God that the Gospel shall ultimately prevail, I answer, Yes, even a general assurance from God we clasp to our hearts. But how much more assuring it would be, if God were so good as to lay before us his plan for the future of the Gospel. And God has been so good.

We learn from the prophecies that the state of things around us is just what was foretold from the beginning; and also, as to what is yet before the church, that atheism and blasphemy and moral corruption will be holding high carnival at the time of the Lord's coming, and the Antichrist, the Colossus of falsehood and crime, shall then be at the acme of his imperial sway; but that then him, the man of sin, the son of perdition, the lawless one, the Lord Jesus shall destroy by the Epiphany of his coming.

Then shall Christ reign, putting all enemies under his feet, and the succession of the redeemed be as the dewdrops daily issuing from the womb of the morning.

Pessimism, you say? No, not pessimism, but optimism of the most effective kind. While recognizing what is patent to every eye, the never-diminishing numerical majority against the Gospel, we yet know God's plan, and we triumph in the assurance of the all-conquering Epiphany of Jesus out of heaven.

Here, then, is history written before. We see the mile-posts of the future. Trees in the great black forests are notched to blaze the way of the coming jubilee of the Gospel. Things are not at loose ends. God's purpose is fixed, his eye watchful, his hand over all. It is our joy of specific knowledge; the joy of partienlarized assurance; a balm for depression, a cordial for our fears. Accordingly, in times of persecution, the Church has always found her refuge in prophecy. With the early Christians in their conflicts with pagan Rome, with the Waldenses in their conflicts with papal Rome, the very service-book, the *vade mecum*, was the Apocalypse. A joy it is to be apprised beforehand of the course of events leading on to victory. We have but to stand in our place, and give our testimony. God will take care of his Gospel.

Another joy of prophecy is that of anticipating completed redemption. What is completed redemption? The salvation of a soul—is that not redemption? Yes, and glorious indeed; still only partial redemption. A whole world of saved sinners, is that not redemption? Yes, and yet more glorious; still only partial redemption. The advancement of all saved sinners to the honors and the glories with which the boundless God may fill the eternal state, is that not redemption? Yes, and more and more glorious; still only partial redemption. For are we to consider man apart from his home? How incongruous, if a drunkard were reformed, and elevated to respectability and dignity, while yet his home were left in the disgraceful condition inflicted by his drunkenness; the house still infested with filth and disorder, the window panes shattered and ragged, the fences broken down, the garden overrun with weeds, unkempt and uncared for. What is home? Is there a forlorner wretch than the man without a home? Now has not earth been fitted up as the home of mankind? When God expended upon it his six days' creation work, arranging it, furnishing it, making it very good, did he mean it for only a temporary abiding place? And when sin came, did it strike the inhabitants only? Didn't it wrench and impair the frame of creation? Even the atmosphere was worsened; for now it made necessary to man the wearing of clothing. In his Edenic state the æsthetics of his soul were inconceivably higher, purer, sweeter, so that the clothing, which is now so much an expression of the beautiful, would have been in that superior condition of being an impertinence, a *smear;* his conceptions of fitness and beauty being so far above the present possibilities of culture, as a Raphael's Madonna the daub of a Hottentot. Man fell not only from holiness into sin, but also, and by consequence, from the heaven of the science of the beautiful into a beggary of thought and feeling. And the point is, that the chill, piercing winds of winter, themselves the result of man's sin, and making clothing a necessity, are ever reminding him of this downward transition, as though they were a sort of human conscience, and themselves a part of the human self. Milton stated it none too strongly:

> "Earth felt the wound, and nature from her seat,
> Sighing through all her works, gave signs of woe
> That all was lost."

And now when redemption came, did it stretch forth the uplifting hand to the inhabitant alone, and not also to the home? Besides, forasmuch as the scenes of inconceivable beauty that draped the unfallen earth were what touched into consummate action the pure æsthetics of unfallen man, it follows that the restitution of earth to at least its original beauty is a condition precedent to regaining for man his lost sense of the beautiful. The redemption of man himself takes along with it the redemption of the earth. Not till then will redemption have been completely realized.

And this is what the Spirit in prophecy authorizes us to anticipate. The creation, he says, groaning and travailing in pain together until now, is waiting, in earnest expectation, for the manifestation of the sons of God; having been made subject to vanity in hope that itself also shall be delivered from the bondage of corruption into the freedom of the glory of the children of God (Rom. 8: 19–22). Thus the inhabitants and their home: the one the reflection of the glorious freedom of the other. So fixed and sure is this purpose of God, the earth and its atmosphere are represented as thrilling with hope, and stretching out the neck in longing to catch the dawning of the day of regeneration. That deliverance will be somewhat as when the worm has become a butterfly: so much more beautiful now than before. Crisp and delightful as is often now our morning air, and charming as are so many landscapes, the earth then shall be so far superior to what it is now. Matter, which ranges from iron ore or granite rock to the imponderable ether pervading the universe, is capable, by the manipulation of God, of taking on a heavenly magnificence. Matter the Eternal Son of God took into personal union with himself, and lo! with a brightness above that of the midday sun it dazzled to blindness Saul of Tarsus. Matter, sown in corruption, shall be raised in incorruption; sown in dishonor, shall be raised in glory; sown in weakness, shall be raised in power; sown an animal body, shall be raised a body with Divine life from the Spirit. And then "the light of the moon shall be as the light of the sun, and the light of the sun shall be seven-fold" (Isa. 30: 26). And yet "the moon shall be confounded and the sun ashamed, when the Lord of hosts shall reign in Mount Zion, and before his ancients gloriously" (Isa. 24: 23). And so "we look for new heavens and a new earth, wherein dwelleth righteousness" (2 Pet. 3: 13). That will be redemption completed.

Now is not this a joy of anticipation congenial to the human soul? next to that of friendship with God, the greatest joy conceivable? Says Dr. Chalmers, in his sermon on the new heavens and the new earth, To think of our future locality as "a lofty aerial region, where the inmates float in ether, or are mysteriously suspended upon nothing, where every vestige of materialism, is done away, certainly tends to abate the interest with which we might otherwise look to the perspective that is on the other side of the grave." "It altogether holds out," he continues, "a warmer and more alluring picture of the elysium that awaits us, when told, that there will be ground to walk upon, beauty to delight the eye, music to regale the ear, smiles that play on the human countenance, accents of kindness that fall in soft and soothing melody from the human voice." It only needs that matter shall be clarified of the evil effects of man's sin, to bring it into heavenly harmony with heavenly man, and to make the earth a heavenly seat of the kingdom of heaven for which we are praying. O joy that warms the heart, that contents us to bear the whips and stings of suffering, that makes heavenly-mindedness attractive!

The joyous mind of the Spirit is the spirit of prophecy.

Finally, the Holy Spirit in prophecy is the promoter of Christian foreign missions.

In one of his most important oracles he foretells that

"this Gospel of the kingdom shall be preached in all the world for a witness unto all nations, and then shall the end come." Not when the Gospel shall have been truly received by all nations, but when it shall have been preached as a witness to them; not when the world shall have been converted, but when it shall have been evangelized. The nearer, then, we are to that great objective point, the evangelizing of all nations, the nearer we are to the end of this world-age; nearer to that revelation of glory, of which the scene on the Mount of Transfiguration was the earnest and demonstration. Not universal success in converting men, but universal activity in calling them to conversion is the crisis of the world's history.

Now what a motive is this for the urgency of aggressive Christian work. The Church's business is to testify the Gospel " whether men will hear, or whether they will forbear." Her success is to be measured, not by the number of her converts, but by the extent and thoroughness of her testimony, and by her taking out of the nations a people for his name (a very little flock it may be), Acts 15 : 14. And grand success it is, even though her converts be not more than as one grain of wheat in a bushel of chaff; for merely by her spread of the Gospel message she is hastening on the day of the Lord.

The heathen may reject the missionary's good tidings in as large numbers as do the evangelized masses of Christendom. The churches at home may grow worldly, the tares everywhere luxuriant, the goats multiplying faster than the sheep. Churchmen may call in question the claims of world-evangelization, and, by statistical figures, which are said, by a grim sarcasm, not to lie, prove to their own satisfaction that missions are a failure. In heathendom, as in Christendom, pride may deify the human intellect; science, so-called, may wag its cerberus heads at the crucified Jesus, and philosophy, perverted, with its Briareus arms, essay to unseat the Lord God Almighty. Discouragement may cloud the prospect to those true-hearted stewards of the Gospel who, unfortunately for themselves, are dwelling in the low valley of unprophetic Christian thought. But to the workers on the mountain top of prophecy, how far-reaching the view, what a horizon of triumph; for when, by God's blessing, in spite of indifference or ridicule, the faithful shall have testified the message amongst all peoples, the Lord Jesus himself shall take care of the rest. He will come, he will come! His arrows shall be sharp in the heart of the King's enemies; going forth conquering and to conquer on behalf of truth and meekness and righteousness.

And how much the sanctified enthusiasm of this prophetic prospect has had to do with the progress and achievement of foreign missions may be seen in such names as Martyn, Wolf, Heber, Gutzlaff, Bettleheim, Duff, J. Hudson Taylor and his 300 missionaries in China, Guinness, Ashley Cooper, Earl of Shaftsbury (*clarum and venerabile nomen*), and others: men, whether in foreign lands, or workers at home for the cause, hot with missionary zeal, and students of prophecy, sympathizers with the mind of the Spirit.

But why speak of lesser names? The greatest missionary of the Christian ages, he who dwelt with rapture on creation's hope of the manifestation of the sons of God; who did not believe that Christian culture and civilization would gradually develop into the millennium, but emphasized the predicted falling away in the professing church, and the perilous times in the last days; who was ever looking for the Epiphany of the Lord's presence, and the miraculous introduction of his kingdom; what were his labors as a foreign missionary? From the falling of the scales off his eyes at Damascus, till he sat behind the grated windows of Nero's prison; whether journeying in deserts, traversing seas, beaten with stones, clanking his chains; whether on the beach at Miletus, or scaling Mount Olympus, or on Mars' Hill, or in a Philippian prison; who can compare with him as to work done and difficulties encountered? At that marvelous recital forced from him by his detractors —" In labors more abundant, in stripes above measure, in prisons more frequent, in deaths oft; of the Jews five times received I forty stripes save one, thrice was I beaten with rods, once was I stoned, thrice I suffered shipwreck, a night and day I have been in the deep; in journeyings often, in perils of waters, in perils of robbers, in perils by mine own countrymen, in perils by the heathen, in perils in the city, in perils in the wilderness, in perils in the sea, in perils among false brethren; in weariness and painfulness, in watchings often, in hunger and thirst, in fastings often, in cold and nakedness"—can we help exclaiming with Erskine in the British Parliament, "Great God, what a salary for a faithful minister!" But his love of Christ and his prophetic faith bore him onward. And triumphantly he carried the Gospel of the kingdom from Antioch to Illyricum, from the Euxine to the pillars of Hercules; and in less than a quarter of a century he had evangelized twenty nations, besides the islands of Cyprus and Crete.

The missionary mind of the Spirit is the spirit of prophecy.

Look back now over this rapid sketch. The spirit of prophecy is a composite of characteristics, Divine and human, a focus of excellencies; for like a sun-glass, prophecy converges to a point the Spirit's rays of light and heat, and sets the soul aflame. The intelligible mind of the Spirit, the instructive mind of the Spirit, the Christly mind of the Spirit, the adorable mind of the Spirit, the holy mind of the Spirit, the joyous mind of the Spirit, the missionary mind of the Spirit, these are the spirit of prophecy. Take away what of the Holy Spirit prophecy gives us, and, comparatively, how little we should know of him. Would we have a livelier enjoyment of his fellowship? O Blessed Spirit of God, who art thyself our patient, gentle, untiring Companion and Friend, by day and by night, without whom never a spiritual consolation felt, never a duty well done, never a trial sweetly borne, never a triumph in death, and by whom not seldom we are rapt into a speechless pleasure of worship, can it be, by this love of thine, that we have the heart to slight what thou hast been at pains to teach us? We hear thee say, "He that hath my Word, let him speak my Word faithfully. What is the chaff to the wheat?" With bowed heads and smitten hearts, reverently, lovingly we answer thee, Amen and Amen!

www.ingramcontent.com/pod-product-compliance
Lightning Source LLC
Chambersburg PA
CBHW050802160426
43192CB00010B/1610